GOLDEN ANSWERS

Why We Need the Book of Mormon

JOHN BYTHEWAY

DESERET BOOK

Salt Lake City, Utah

Library of Congress Cataloging-in-Publication Data

Names: Bytheway, John, 1962– author.

Title: Golden answers : why we need The Book of Mormon / John Bytheway.

Description: Salt Lake City, Utah : Deseret Book, [2020] | Includes bibliographical references. | Summary: "Author John Bytheway explains why the Book of Mormon is essential to our understanding of the gospel of Jesus Christ"— Provided by publisher.

Identifiers: LCCN 2019041842 | ISBN 9781629727257 (trade paperback)

Subjects: LCSH: The Church of Jesus Christ of Latter-day Saints—Doctrines. | Book of Mormon—Criticism, interpretation, etc. | Spiritual life—The Church of Jesus Christ of Latter-day Saints. | Spiritual life—Mormon Church. | Christian life—Mormon authors. | Plan of salvation (Mormon theology) | Mormon Church—Doctrines.

Classification: LCC BX8656 .B98 2020 | DDC 230/.93—dc23

LC record available at https://lccn.loc.gov/2019041842

Printed in the United States of America

PubLitho, Draper, UT

10 9 8 7 6 5 4 3 2 1

CONTENTS

Chapter One

I'M THIRSTY; WHERE DID YOU GET THAT?

"This may be the most important class you will ever take," I often begin. "Not because of your instructor," I continue, "but because of our textbook. Thankfully, we will not be judged by the material in our biology textbook, or our history textbook, or our macroeconomics textbook (thank heavens), but we when we face the final judgment, *this* book, the Book of Mormon, will be mentioned by the Lord himself when he asks, 'Did I not declare my words unto you, which were written by this man, like as one crying from the dead, yea, even as one speaking out of the dust?' (Moroni 10:27)."

I have recently had the opportunity to teach a relatively new class, which in institute of religion lingo is called "Religion 275." In this class, rather than teaching the Book of Mormon by starting in 1 Nephi and going chapter by chapter through Moroni 10, we focus on *Doctrines and Teachings of the Book of Mormon.*

At first, I confess that I thought, "Here we go again with yet another way of doing things, and how am I supposed to condense all of this into one semester?"

However, I scrapped my old lesson plans and began to read and research and create new ones. After a few weeks, I found myself repenting and thanking heaven for this new approach. I discovered again, and appreciated more than ever before, the uniqueness and the clarifying power of the Book of Mormon.

As a teacher, I have been humbled and grateful for the young and curious students who have entered my classroom. On the first day of class, I always ask them to stand and introduce themselves to each other. I invite them to share some biographical information, like where they live, their missionary service, if any, and something fun, like their favorite fast-food restaurant (In-N-Out usually wins, by the way). They come from all over the country and have served all over the world.

As we begin on the first day, I often introduce the course by asking my well-traveled students, "Does water taste different in different parts of the country, or in different parts of the world?" Everyone answers with an affirmative nod or a spoken "Yes."

We then begin a discussion on the importance of water, arguably the most vital substance on earth. How long can one survive without water? Only a few days. Scientists have a probe or two on the planet Mars right now. What are they looking for? Water. Because if there is water, there could be life!

At this point, I try to introduce my own little parable (which is not all that profound, as parables go, but here it is):

A wandering traveler, lost, thirsty, and desperate, discovered a beautiful mountain lake. He excitedly dropped his belongings on the shore, got on his hands and knees, and drank the lifesaving liquid deeply and gratefully. As he swallowed the cool water, he felt it soothe his parched throat, restore his energy, and bolster his spirit. Then he rolled onto his back, closed his eyes, and sighed in gratitude.

Suddenly, he discovered he was not alone, as a man who lived near the waters approached him quietly and asked, "Do you know why this water tastes so good?"

"Yes," the weary traveler replied, "because I had been without water for so long, and I was very thirsty."

"Indeed," answered the man, "but there's more. Look over there," he gestured, and as the traveler looked toward the east, he saw a vast mountain range and a stream flowing from it into the lake. "The stream from those mountains gives the water its minerals and rich taste. Now look over to the other side. What do you see?" The traveler looked west and saw a small waterfall forming another river, which fed the lake from the west. "That tributary gives this water its coolness and freshness. But that's not all," the man continued. "This lake is also fed by a spring that you cannot see. And in certain seasons, as heavy clouds approach these mountains, they release their abundant moisture, creating a runoff that keeps the lake full to overflowing. This body of water would be diminished without any one of them. Each of these sources contributes to the beauty of the lake and the quality of this pure, refreshing liquid."

"Thank you. I really didn't know any of that until

now, and I probably wouldn't have thought of it unless you explained it," replied the traveler. "All I know is that it was delicious to me. It renewed my soul, filled me with hope, and gave me exactly what I needed." Then the traveler paused for a moment and continued, "But after today, I will respect and appreciate everything connected to this lake. Not only is it the best water I've ever tasted, but it saved my life."

So there's my amateur parable. You probably already know where I'm going with this, which is the nice thing about parables. Elder David A. Bednar taught:

> The scriptures contain the words of Christ and are a reservoir of living water to which we have ready access and from which we can drink deeply and long. ("A Reservoir of Living Water," BYU Devotional, February 4, 2007)

We might call our own testimonies and gospel knowledge our "personal reservoir." For the most part, my young adult students know the fundamentals of the gospel. They have a good-sized reservoir of gospel knowledge. They've heard countless Primary and Sunday School lessons, seminary classes, and *Come, Follow Me* lessons. But what is the source, the *primary source,* for all of this knowledge? (If there's one thing I remember from my master's program in Religious Education, it was to always go to primary sources—they drummed it into us every day.) The source material for all these teachings that comprise our reservoir are the revelations from the Lord, or, in other words, the scriptures.

In class, when we discuss a certain doctrine or principle of the gospel, one of my favorite questions to ask is, "Okay, where do we get that? I don't mean who taught you that in the past, but where—in our most important source documents—where do we get that?"

As this particular class unfolds (Religion 275), I want the students to discover and appreciate how much of the living water we drink every day comes from what my parable referred to as the river on the west, or, in other words, the Book of Mormon. The tributary on the east, the Holy Bible, is rich and beautiful and absolutely necessary for our lake of living water. Our lake would be incomplete without it. The spring, the Light of Christ or the Holy Ghost, teaches us daily, and the rains of revelation have come frequently ever since Joseph knelt in the Sacred Grove. But the Book of Mormon, carefully crafted and designed for our day, is stunningly relevant to our modern situation. Sometimes, as we come to realize how much the Book of Mormon contributes to our gospel knowledge, I can see the lights go on in students' heads. (One student, discovering a new insight in the Book of Mormon, looked at his classmate and gave him the "mind blown" gesture. One of my favorite rewards for being a teacher is seeing my students grow in their love and appreciation for the scriptures.

To provide further motivation for my class members to go from "casual readers" to "serious students," I sometimes ask them to imagine how powerful it would be if we could invite Lucy Mack Smith to address us as we begin the course. What would she say? Perhaps she might ask, "Do you know what it cost my family to bring you this book?" The answer to her question is heart wrenching, even heartbreaking. And yet, her family and many others made the sacrifice to place this treasure in our hands.

I have always loved this statement of President Spencer W. Kimball:

> Sometimes it seems we take the scriptures too much for granted because we do not fully appreciate how rare a thing it is to possess them, and how blessed we are because we do have them. We seem to have settled so comfortably into our experiences in this world and become so accustomed to hearing the gospel taught among us that it is hard for us to imagine it could ever have been otherwise. ("How Rare a Possession—the Scriptures!" *Ensign*, September 1976)

As a member of the Church who grew up always having a set of scriptures, I find it hard to imagine what life would be like without them, or what it would be like to live in a time when you were forbidden to read them. In fact, if I could offer a homework assignment here, I might suggest watching the video *How Rare a Possession*, which features the Book of Mormon and its role in the conversion of Parley P. Pratt and Vincenzo di Francesca. As you watch, feel what they felt as these men who thirsted for truth tasted this living water for the very first time. Your appreciation for the Book of Mormon and the power within its verses will grow.

The purpose of this little book is to assist you in your

study to answer these questions: Why do we need the Book of Mormon? What did this product of the Restoration restore? What doctrine does it clarify, and what doctrine does it affirm? Obviously, we cannot cover all the doctrine and principles taught, but I have chosen some of my favorites—golden answers to golden questions from the golden plates.

Chapter Two

A SECOND WITNESS OF CHRIST—AND MUCH MORE

One morning, I caught my students by surprise as I flipped the switch on the projection screen (which is almost always in the lowered position) and watched it ascend into its secret compartment in the ceiling while I hunted for a dry-erase marker in front of an empty whiteboard. Though we all love PowerPoint presentations, there is nothing like a good ol' chalkboard or whiteboard for getting a discussion going. With a fresh marker in hand, I began class with what I thought was a very simple question: Why do we need the Book of Mormon?

A hand shot up, and someone responded, "It is a second witness for Christ."

"Yes it is! That is an important answer, practically lifted from the title page," I said as I wrote it on the board. The front cover itself describes the book as "Another Testament of Jesus Christ." Then I turned around and asked, "But what if someone says, 'I don't need another witness; I already believe in Christ'?"

That's when things got quiet. So we sat in silence for a minute. Then the question became, "What then, specifically, does the Book of Mormon give us that is not in the Old or New Testament?" The silence was compounded by blank stares. (As an educator, I love blank stares—it means we get to fill in the blanks!)

If the Book of Mormon were *only* a second witness for Christ, then it could be just the same stuff, different continent. But the Book of Mormon is more. The book expands, explains, and clarifies. It also validates many biblical stories and personalities and defends the truthfulness of the Bible. In fact, Elder Tad R. Callister taught, "Again and again the Book of Mormon acts as a confirming, clarifying, unifying witness of the doctrines taught in the Bible" ("The Book of Mormon—a Book from God," *Ensign*, November 2011).

If we're going to flood the earth with the Book of Mormon, we ought to have a clear idea of what's in it and why the Lord wanted us to have it. We ought to know not only that it is another testament of Jesus Christ; we ought to know how it expounds the gospel of Jesus Christ in wonderful ways.

SAVIOR OF THE WHOLE WORLD

When our class reached this point, some deeper thinking began. "Well," one student said, "it shows that Jesus Christ cares about the whole world, not just those in one place."

Yes! The Book of Mormon is intensely Christ-centered, and he is the Savior of the whole world in both hemispheres. The Savior is referenced by one of his many names or titles an average of every 1.7 verses in the Book of Mormon (see Susan Ward Easton, "Names of Christ in the

Book of Mormon," *Ensign,* July 1978). In other words, on average, you can't read two verses in the Book of Mormon without a mention of Christ.

The major purposes of the Book of Mormon are explained on its title page:

1. "Show unto the remnant of the house of Israel what great things the Lord hath done for their fathers."
2. "That they may know the covenants of the Lord, that they are not cast off forever."
3. "To the convincing of the Jew and Gentile that Jesus is the Christ, the Eternal God, manifesting himself unto all nations."

My student made a good point. One of the phrases on the title page that stands out to me is "unto *all* nations." If Jesus Christ really is the God of the whole earth, and he is, then we should not be surprised that he would manifest himself unto *all* nations. The Lord himself expands on the "unto all nations" idea with power:

> Know ye not that there are more nations than one? Know ye not that I, the Lord your God, have created all men, and that I remember those who are upon the isles of the sea; and that I rule in the heavens above and in the earth beneath; and I bring forth my word unto the children of men, yea, even upon all the nations of the earth? (2 Nephi 29:7)

While the majority of the Christian world maintains that the canon of scriptures is closed, the Latter-day Saints are waiting for more. Who has the authority (or the audacity) to tell God to stop talking? Who can impose a vow of silence on God or tell him to stop speaking to his children in overt, literal ways? Not only will more revelation come, but we cannot stop it.

> As well might man stretch forth his puny arm to stop the Missouri river in its decreed course, or to turn it up stream, as to hinder the Almighty from pouring down knowledge from heaven upon the heads of the Latter-day Saints. (D&C 121:33)

The very existence of the Book of Mormon is a testimony that God continues to communicate with his children.

DEFENDER OF THE BIBLE

Why else do we need the Book of Mormon? Another student suggested that the Book of Mormon verifies the stories of Jesus found in other scriptures. Yes! If you read closely, you will hear the Book of Mormon defending the Bible!

As members of the Church, we know that the Book of Mormon cannot and does not replace the Bible. In fact, the Book of Mormon vigorously defends the importance and truthfulness of the Bible! The Bible and the Book of Mormon are not rivals. They are companion volumes that combine to testify of Christ. Some of Mormon's very last words to future generations testify of the Bible's truthfulness:

> Therefore repent, and be baptized in the name of Jesus, and lay hold upon the gospel of Christ, which shall be set before you, not only in this record but also

in the record which shall come unto the Gentiles from the Jews [the Bible], which record shall come from the Gentiles unto you. For behold, this [the Book of Mormon] is written for the intent that ye may believe that [the Bible]; and if ye believe that [the Bible] ye will believe this [the Book of Mormon] also; and if ye believe this ye will know concerning your fathers, and also the marvelous works which were wrought by the power of God among them. (Mormon 7:8–9)

Not only does the Book of Mormon defend the Bible, but the Lord chastises the people of the world for their treatment of those who worked and sacrificed to bring the Bible to them:

And what thank they the Jews for the Bible which they receive from them? Yea, what do the Gentiles mean? Do they remember the travails, and the labors, and the pains of the Jews, and their diligence unto me, in bringing forth salvation unto the Gentiles? O ye Gentiles, have ye remembered the Jews, mine ancient covenant people? Nay; but ye have cursed them, and have hated them, and have not sought to recover them. But behold, I will return all these things upon your own heads; for I the Lord have not forgotten my people. (2 Nephi 29:4–5)

In addition, the Book of Mormon fulfills what has been called the law of witnesses, that "in the mouth of two or three witnesses every word may be established" (Matthew 18:16; see also Deuteronomy 19:15; John 8:12–19). The Bible and the Book of Mormon are dual witnesses of Christ.

DEFENDER OF BIBLE STORIES

Another student commented, "The Book of Mormon verifies a lot of Bible stories that some people think are only fables."

Some Christians doubt that there really was a Garden of Eden, a tower of Babel, an ark built by Noah, and so forth, believing these accounts to be only allegorical. The Book of Mormon validates the biblical account of Adam and Eve (2 Nephi 2) and mentions Noah and the ark (Alma 10:22; Ether 6:7), the tower of Babel (Omni 1:22; Mosiah 28:17; Helaman 6:28; Ether 1:3), Melchizedek (Alma 13:14–19), and Moses and the brazen serpent (Helaman 8:11–16). Interestingly, the Book of Mormon adds one important detail to Moses's story—it testifies that as Moses raised the brazen serpent, he explicitly bore testimony "that the Son of God should come" (Helaman 8:14)—a fascinating prophecy and foreshadowing of Christ that does not appear in the Old Testament account (see Numbers 21:8–9).

DEFENDER OF THE DIVINITY OF CHRIST

There's something else that most of us have never thought of, and that is that the Book of Mormon affirms the divinity of Christ. My students have asked, "Doesn't every Christian denomination affirm Christ's divinity?" Actually, no. Just as there is a broad spectrum of belief in political matters, from liberal to conservative, there is also a broad spectrum of belief in Christian doctrine. In my graduate studies in Religious Education, I was surprised to learn that many Bible scholars are not necessarily Bible believers, and that some liberal Christians believe Jesus to be merely a great moral teacher, not the divine Son of God. Some also discount miracles and prophecy and dispute the authorship of many books within the Bible.

The late 1980s saw the introduction of the "Jesus Seminar," a conference of liberal Christians, scholars, and ministers who concluded (among other things) that Jesus did not really deliver the Sermon on the Mount, did not speak about his flesh and blood at the Last Supper, did not predict his own death and resurrection, and never claimed to be the Son of God. They threw out most of the book of John. The net effect was to declare Jesus's teachings to be nothing more than a collection of philosophical ideas, with no power to save.

More recently, many books and articles speak of the search for the "historical Jesus," a phrase that usually describes the effort to diminish or remove anything "supernatural" from the biblical text, such as miracles or prophecies, in an effort to get down to the "real," or "historical," Jesus.

By contrast, the Book of Mormon declares Jesus Christ to be the divine Son of God on the title page and on practically every page thereafter! President Ezra Taft Benson commented:

> The first and most central theme of the Book of Mormon is that Jesus is the promised Messiah, our Lord and Redeemer. He came to redeem mankind from a lost and fallen condition brought about by Adam's transgression. Nearly all Christian churches accepted this

truth as fundamental to their faith when the Book of Mormon was published to the world in 1830. The fact that another book had come forth as a second witness to Christ's divinity was regarded by many churches as being both superfluous and spurious. They said, "We already have a Bible, why do we need another?" (2 Nephi 29:3).

But the nineteenth century was not the twentieth. Who but God and inspired prophets could have foreseen the need for an additional witness for the divinity of His Son. . . . Who but God and inspired prophets could have foreseen the day when ministers of prominent denominations would openly challenge the divinity of Jesus Christ. (*The Teachings of Ezra Taft Benson* [1988], 49–50)

The ancient prophets who compiled the Book of Mormon must have known that Jesus's divinity as the Son of God and the miracles he performed would one day be discounted or even discarded.

WRITTEN FOR OUR DAY

"The Book of Mormon was written for our day," another student suggested. Yes, it is. In fact, the Book of Mormon writers sometimes directly address the reader (much more directly than the Bible does), using pointed phrases such as, "I speak unto you as if ye were present, and yet ye are not. But behold, Jesus Christ hath shown you unto me, and I know your doing" (Mormon 8:35). These prophets must have seen the future in visions, and they speak to our day and our challenges.

The Bible is like a journal for the house of Israel, a record of God's dealings with the Old Testament prophets, and the New Testament Apostles' testimonies of Christ's ministry, as well as epistles to early Church members and leaders. The twenty-seven books that make up the canon of the New Testament weren't even assembled until the fourth century AD. The Bible authors chronicled events in their day, and we love reading their testimonies.

The Book of Mormon, on the other hand, was written specifically for our day, the latter days, by prophets who saw us and tailored their messages specifically for us. President Ezra Taft Benson observed:

> [The Book of Mormon] was written for our day. The Nephites never had the book, neither did the Lamanites of ancient times. It was meant for us. Mormon wrote near the end of the Nephite civilization. Under the inspiration of God, who sees all things from the beginning, he abridged centuries of records, choosing the stories, speeches, and events that would be most helpful to us. (*Teachings of Ezra Taft Benson,* 58)

Modern readers of the Book of Mormon can't help but notice the repeated messages against pride and immorality and can readily see that the message is pointed to our modern world. Hugh Nibley once commented, "Woe to the generation that understands this book!" (*The World and the Prophets* [1987], 214).

IN SHORT . . .

By the time this little exercise in our Book of Mormon class was over (and it felt like exercise, I might add), we had filled our dry-erase board with many ideas that we could use throughout the semester. Among them, we noted that the Book of Mormon

- Talks about the plan of salvation, the plan of happiness, the plan of redemption.
- Doesn't only command people to repent, but contains stories showing exactly how someone goes through the process of repenting.
- Teaches the necessity of baptism and the practice of the sacrament
- Talks in detail about the Resurrection.
- Teaches how justice and mercy can be satisfied by the Atonement of Jesus Christ.

Once the class got going, comments flowed, and we began to appreciate in some detail how the Book of Mormon confirms some biblical teachings and clarifies others. Again, the Book of Mormon is not a rival, a replacement, or a revision of the Bible. It is a companion, a defender, and a second witness of Jesus Christ, a testimony that God remembers his children in all nations, and that he has not stopped working in our behalf.

Bonus assignment: In the October 2017 general conference, President Russell M. Nelson shared a more comprehensive list in which he outlined what the Book of Mormon *affirms, refutes, fulfills, clarifies,* and *reveals.* His full list can be found at the end of his talk, "The Book of Mormon: What Would Your Life Be Like without It?" Check it out on your Gospel Library app!

Chapter Three

GOD HAS A PLAN

On another day in class, following the opening prayer (which is most importantly a time to ask for help from the Lord, but also serves as a brief moment in which every student takes a break from his or her phone), I asked the students to open the Gospel Library app on their phones or tablets. "Now, go to Scriptures," I said, "touch the little magnifying glass below, and search for a very simple word: *plan*. Ready for a surprise?"

Together we discovered that there are only three uses of the word *plan* in the Old Testament, and there are none—that's right, *none*—in the New Testament. The three Old Testament uses of the word *plan* are actually not in the scriptural text itself but in the synopses, the short, italicized chapter summaries before the text of the scriptures begins. These three references refer to Esau's plan, the Ammonites' plan, and Haman's plan, but there is nothing about God's plan. "Wait a minute," you might ask, "doesn't the Christian world use the phrase *plan of salvation?*" Yes, all the time. But it's not biblical (at least not in the King James Version).

By contrast, the word *plan* appears in the Book of

Mormon sixty-two times, more than two dozen of which describe the plan of salvation. Is the absence of the word *plan* in the Bible just a quirk of translation? Or is it something more?

The Book of Mormon teaches that God has a plan. We exist as part of a plan and a purpose, and that plan was determined in the premortal existence before the world was created.

God didn't have to come up with an "alternate plan" after Adam and Eve fell, because the Fall of man was part of the plan too. (Stay tuned—the Fall is the subject of the next chapter.) Dr. Hugh Nibley suggested that the idea of a plan had

> no place in conventional Christian and Jewish theology, having been vigorously condemned by the doctors of both religions in the fourth and fifth centuries, since they would not tolerate any concepts involving preexistence of the spirit of man. Hence is found the studious avoidance of such words as "plan" and "probation" in our translations of the Bible. (*Since Cumorah* [1981], 188)

The plan of salvation is implied in such biblical verses as, "As in Adam all die, even so in Christ shall all be made alive" (1 Corinthians 15:22) and "He became the author of eternal salvation unto all them that obey him" (Hebrews 5:9), but the idea of a plan is not specifically laid out. By contrast, the Book of Mormon uses *the plan of salvation*, along with many similar phrases meaning the same thing, throughout the text. For example:

"Great and eternal plan" (Alma 34:16)

"Great plan of happiness" (Alma 42:8)

"Great plan of redemption" (Jacob 6:8; Alma 34:31)

"Plan of deliverance" (2 Nephi 11:5)

"Plan of mercy" (Alma 42:15, 31)

"Plan of our God" (2 Nephi 9:13)

"Plan of redemption" (Alma 12:25, 26, 30, 32, 33;
    17:16; 18:39; 22:13; 29:2; 39:18; 42:11, 13)

"Plan of restoration" (Alma 41:2)

"Plan of salvation" (Jarom 1:2; Alma 24:14; 42:5)

"Plan of the Eternal God" (Alma 34:9)

"Plan of the great Creator" (2 Nephi 9:6)

As you can see, the most frequent phrase used to describe the plan of salvation in the Book of Mormon is actually *plan of redemption*. Isn't it interesting that it is used most often by Alma and the sons of Mosiah, who were well aware that they needed *redemption* after they had gone about "seeking to destroy the church" of God (Mosiah 27:10).

Other Restoration scriptures also show that there has always been a divine plan and purpose for everything that God does. In what has often been called the Lord's "mission statement," the Lord taught Moses, "For behold, this is my work and my glory—to bring to pass the immortality and eternal life of man" (Moses 1:39). That's the plan.

THE HISTORY OF THE WORLD HAS ALREADY BEEN WRITTEN

Why is it important to know that God has a plan? Well, just imagine if there were no plan! Sir Isaac Newton wondered if God had simply created everything, set things in motion, and then walked away to let things take their course, governed by the laws of nature. This "Clockwork Universe Theory," that God just wound up the universe like a clock and then adopted a "hands-off" policy and let it run, leaves creation without a purpose and ultimate end. But the scriptures teach that God had a reason and purpose for it all.

God's purposes and his foreknowledge are made particularly clear in the Book of Mormon. For example, Zenos's allegory of the olive tree (see Jacob 5) shows that there has always been a plan for the history of the world. The four visits of the master and the "long times" in between all correspond with historical periods of prophets and apostasy. In addition, Moses, Enoch (Moses 7:67), Nephi (1 Nephi 14:24–25), the brother of Jared, and of course John the Revelator had visions in which they saw the history of the world from beginning to end. If there is a plan, then there is a Planner. And if there is a Planner, then there is a purpose. We are children of God, and our Father has a plan. We are not, as someone once said, an "accidental arrangement of atoms."

The fact that God is at the helm, that he has a plan and a purpose, is a great comfort and also provides us with perhaps the ultimate "no-brainer." Elder Jeffrey R. Holland taught:

> The future of this world has long been declared; the final outcome between good and evil is already known. There is absolutely no question as to who wins because the final victory has already been posted on the scoreboard. The only really strange thing in all of this is that we are still down here on the field trying to decide

which team's jersey we want to wear! (Email correspondence from Jeffrey R. Holland to author, June 1, 2004)

The plan answers man's most universal questions: "Where did I come from?" "Why am I here?" and "What will happen to me when I die?" Our knowledge of God's plan teaches us "which jersey to wear" and encourages us to align our will with the plan of a loving God who wants to bring to pass our immortality and eternal life (see Moses 1:39).

JESUS CHRIST IS THE CENTER OF THE PLAN

Perhaps you've heard it taught that while we were in the premortal existence, two plans were presented. I suppose it could be expressed that way, but, to be more precise, there was really only one plan, which was our Heavenly Father's plan. Satan tried to amend the Father's plan, to the extent that he "sought to destroy the agency of man" (Moses 4:3). It's helpful to remember that the Father's question was "Whom shall I send?" not "What should I do?" (see Abraham 3:27). Jesus Christ became the center of the Father's plan of salvation when he volunteered to be our Savior and Redeemer, and that's when the "gospel of God" became the "gospel of Jesus Christ." Elder Bruce R. McConkie taught:

That plan is the gospel of God, known to us as the gospel of Jesus Christ because he is the one chosen to put all of its terms and conditions into operation. (*The Millennial Messiah: The Second Coming of the Son of Man* [1982], 660)

Occasionally, we attempt to capture the wonder of the plan by drawing diagrams composed of circles, lines, dotted lines, and arrows depicting the various stages of our immortal journey. But the plan of salvation isn't just places we go, it's whom we worship and who remakes us.

One time, I fell victim to a clever religion teacher who embarrassed me in front of the class. I'll never forget the lesson (although I decided I would never do to another student what he did to me). "Draw the plan of salvation on the board," I was instructed, so I did. I drew a circle, a cloud, another circle, a split circle, three more circles, another cloud, a bunch of lines and a few arrows, just as I had seen a number of times. Once everything was labeled, from premortal existence on the top left to outer darkness on the bottom right, I thought I was done.

The teacher looked at my chart and asked, "Where is Christ?" Oops. I gulped and blushed, looking back at what I had drawn, hoping, I suppose, that something might appear. Well, I knew that Christ is central to everything, and that the plan fails without him. Circles and shapes are a lot easier to draw, of course, but I hadn't even thought of drawing Jesus on my diagram. His presence is implied, isn't it? Needless to say, I'll never make that mistake again. Lesson learned.

My teacher was right. A flowchart of geometric shapes misses the most important element of the plan—Jesus Christ. Jesus is the Redeemer within the plan of redemption who makes possible the forgiveness of sin, the spiritual rebirth, and the Resurrection from the dead. (Remember this the next time someone asks you to draw the plan.)

SO WHAT'S THE PLAN?

Brother Robert J. Matthews gave a concise description of the basic elements of the plan when he explained:

> The plan of God calls for a creation, a fall that brings two kinds of death, a probationary period, a set of commandments and ordinances, an infinite atonement by a God, a resurrection, a judgment, and an assignment to one's everlasting destiny. It would destroy the plan if any part or any step were changed or omitted (see Alma 42:8). The plan is a package—none of it is superfluous, none is optional. (*A Bible! A Bible!* [1990], 175)

Man's plans often fail. God's plan will not. When we mortals make plans, we have to see them through, and we often run into obstacles and have to make a "change of plans." Someone has even joked that if you want to make God laugh, make plans.

God's plan is different, since he is perfect and knows the future. Some may ask, "Well, if God already knows what I'm going to do and where I'm going to end up, why doesn't he just send me there now?" I suppose that's because he wants us to experience it ourselves. If we just skipped our probationary state, it would deny us of the growth we would receive by going through mortality. The Lord said, "We will prove them herewith, to see if they will do all things whatsoever the Lord their God shall command them" (Abraham 3:25). So the Lord will "prove us," and we will also "prove" to ourselves what kind of people we want to be.

President Hugh B. Brown was once asked why God required Abraham to sacrifice Isaac, since he already knew that Abraham would be willing to do it. President Brown answered, "Abraham needed to learn something about Abraham" (Truman G. Madsen, *Joseph Smith the Prophet* [1989], 93). In the same way, we will go through our eternal journey, learn through our own experience to discern truth and error, and one day know for ourselves and acknowledge before God, "Thy judgments are just" (see Mosiah 16:1).

WHICH CAME FIRST, THE COMMANDMENTS OR THE PLAN?

The plan of salvation gives a framework for understanding every other doctrine of the gospel. The plan of salvation supplies the "why" behind each of the commandments. The plan is the "big picture" within which every "little picture" makes sense. Alma taught the people of Ammonihah:

> Therefore, God gave unto them commandments, *after* having made known unto them the plan of redemption. (Alma 12:32; emphasis added)

The word *after* indicates a sequence, and if we reversed the phrases, it would say "God made known unto them the plan of redemption [and then] gave unto them commandments." In other words, the plan of salvation was lesson one. It was taught first and foremost. Only after the plan is understood do the commandments make sense. The plan of salvation teaches choices and consequences and explains

how "wickedness never was happiness" (Alma 41:10). Add
to that modern revelation, and we learn the purpose of eternal families and why, as Elder Mark E. Petersen once said,
"Humanity will rise or fall through its attitude toward the
law of chastity" (in Conference Report, April 1969, 62).

If we teach the commandments without teaching the
plan of salvation, the gospel may seem like nothing but a
long list of dos and don'ts without a context, a design, or an
ultimate purpose. Sadly, some see religion that way, as just a
bunch of random rules with no reasons. But President Boyd
K. Packer taught that knowledge of the plan is a protection:

> Without a knowledge of the gospel plan, transgression
> seems natural, innocent, even justified. There is no greater
> protection from the adversary than for us to know the
> truth—to know the plan! (*Our Father's Plan* [1984], 27)

The book of Jarom within the Book of Mormon has
only one chapter. Interestingly, Jarom's brief record was
brief because he knew the plan had already been taught:
"For what could I write more than my fathers have written? For have not they revealed the plan of salvation? I say
unto you, Yea; and this sufficeth me" (Jarom 1:2). Good
enough. It sufficeth me too.

WHAT THE RESTORATION RESTORED

So what does the Book of Mormon teach us concerning our purpose on earth? Well, it teaches us repeatedly that
God has a plan—a plan described as a plan of redemption,
a plan of deliverance, a plan of mercy, and a plan of happiness. It teaches us of the Fall of Adam and the Atonement of

Jesus Christ and the Resurrection of all mankind (which will be covered in more detail in subsequent chapters).

Occasionally, as we ponder the plan of redemption, we may wonder if all of this could have been done another way. Whenever I try to comprehend the depths of the Savior's suffering, I have wondered the same thing. Couldn't there have been another way to do this? Couldn't there have been a way that the most perfect person who ever lived wouldn't have to have the infinite weight of the sins of all mankind press upon him with such intensity that he bled at every pore? Even Jesus, it seems, wondered at that point if there was another way when he asked, "if it be possible, let this cup pass from me" (Matthew 26:39).

Well, I have a fallback verse in the Book of Mormon—the one verse I go to when all of my "whys" end up with no answer. That verse is 2 Nephi 2:24. It's not long, but it's the verse I turn to when I'm stumped about why God is doing things the way he does them.

Lehi told his son Jacob, "All things have been done in the wisdom of him who knoweth all things" (2 Nephi 2:24). In other words, someone infinitely smarter than I am came up with the plan, and everything is unfolding as it should. There is a plan, a merciful plan, a plan of deliverance, and you and I and all the people on earth have a place in God's eternal plan. This is his work and his glory, and, as he said, "I am able to do mine own work" (2 Nephi 27:21). Whether visible or not in our blackboard depictions, the Book of Mormon testifies that there is a plan characterized by such powerful words as *redemption, mercy,* and *happiness,* and Jesus Christ is the center of that plan.

Chapter Four

THE FORTUNATE FALL

True confessions time—I am a bargain shopper. In fact, you'll find me at the Deseret Industries store about once a week. "What are you looking for there?" you ask. You'll find me hovering around the book section. I am trying to build the type of library my dad built. Occasionally, I find some of my own books there (which says something about my writing, but I'd rather not think about it too long). One time I found one of my books, one that I had authored, in nearly new condition. When I opened the front cover, I was surprised to find that I had autographed it and given it to a member of my ward! So I bought it for a dollar and took it home. When I showed my wife, we both laughed; then she said, "Let's give it to 'em again!" Then we laughed harder.

Someone recently gave me a gift card to Barnes and Noble bookstore (which doesn't sell used books), so, bargain shopper that I am, I went straight to the sale tables. There I found a book with the intriguing title *The Worst Decisions Ever! History's Biggest Mistakes and the People Who Made Them,* by Stephen Weir. The front cover depicted the Titanic as it sank into the icy sea. I thought, "This might be interesting," so I bought it. The first sentence of the number-one "worst decision ever" said this:

> The original idiots, the ones responsible, apparently,
> for all the idiocy that came after them, were the first two
> humans: Adam and Eve. (*Worst Decisions Ever* [2017], 8)

When I share this with my students, a few jaws drop. Some of them are not aware of how Adam and Eve are perceived by many in the Christian world. Some months earlier, I bought a book called *Who's Who in the Bible,* a Reader's Digest publication. I was particularly interested in what it would say about Melchizedek, but when I read the entry about Eve, I grimaced at this final thought:

> In later Christian theology, Eve was called the devil's
> gateway and was often seen as the negative counterpart
> to Mary, the mother of Jesus. (*Who's Who in the Bible*
> [1994], 109)

Where did these conclusions come from? Almost every class session, I begin by asking my students, "Now, what's the title of this class again?" and my students roll their eyes and answer, "Doctrines and Teachings of the Book of Mormon." "Right," I reply, and then I direct them to open their scriptures or their Gospel Library app. "What if the only information we had about the Fall of man came from the Bible? Let's search the Topical Guide and see what we have." There are only seven references, the first three in Genesis as the event unfolds, and the last four all in the epistles of Paul. We read every reference in a classroom setting, but for our purposes here, let's just read the last two:

But I fear, lest by any means, as the serpent be-
guiled Eve through his subtilty, so your minds should
be corrupted from the simplicity that is in Christ.
(2 Corinthians 11:3)

Let the woman learn in silence with all subjection.
But I suffer not a woman to teach, nor to usurp authority over the man, but to be in silence. For Adam was
first formed, then Eve. And Adam was not deceived,
but the woman being deceived was in the transgression.
Notwithstanding she shall be saved in childbearing, if
they continue in faith and charity and holiness with so-
briety. (1 Timothy 2:11–15)

As you might imagine, these verses can be a little un-
settling, as they have been for the Christian world, without
some inspired commentary and clarification. Permit one
additional example of how Adam and Eve are perceived
from Brother Robert L. Millet:

I was driving across the country, listening to the car
radio as I traveled. I especially enjoy listening to religious channels and networks to better understand the
perspective of our Protestant and Catholic friends. On
one channel the host of a rather popular program was
taking calls from the listening audience, soliciting religious questions. One caller asked, "Reverend, why did
Adam and Eve take the fruit of the tree of the knowledge of good and evil?" The minister's answer was
simple. "I don't know," he said. "That's the dumbest
thing anyone could have done! Why, if Adam and Eve
had not been so selfish, so power-hungry, we might all
have been in paradise today!" The answer at the time

caused me to chuckle. I have since thought again and again about his answer and looked more soberly and sympathetically upon a Christian world which desperately needs what we as Latter-day Saints have to offer. ("Adam, A Latter-day Perspective," in *The Man Adam,* ed. Joseph Fielding McConkie and Robert L. Millet [1990], 190)

So what do we, as Latter-day Saints, have to offer? The Book of Mormon, for one thing, and, more specifically, a few words from Father Lehi to his son Jacob. These few verses are a fountain of theological freshwater into our gospel reservoir. Remember that Jacob had never seen Jerusalem—he was born in the wilderness and raised in a family in the midst of extremely trying circumstances, having experienced the "rudeness" of his brothers in his tender years (2 Nephi 2:1). How fitting, then, that Lehi would teach Jacob about the necessity of "opposition in all things" (2 Nephi 2:11) and the event that brought it all about. These verses are so important, and so concise, that I worry my students will breeze through them too quickly:

> And now, behold, if Adam had not transgressed he would not have fallen, but he would have remained in the garden of Eden. And all things which were created must have remained in the same state in which they were after they were created; and they must have remained forever, and had no end. And they would have had no children; wherefore they would have remained in a state of innocence, having no joy, for they knew no misery; doing no good, for they knew no sin. (2 Nephi 2:22–23)

The kind of growth Adam and Eve needed would not have been possible had they remained in the garden, and the kind of growth and experiences we needed could not have happened, because Adam and Eve "would have had no children"! A concluding verse of Lehi's thought is one of the most repeated verses in the Book of Mormon: "Adam fell that men might be; and men are, that they might have joy" (2 Nephi 2:25).

How do these insights change our understanding of Adam and Eve and of the Fall? They teach us that the Fall was definitely downward, yes, but also forward. Thus it is often called a "fortunate fall." (The first person to use the phrase *fortunate fall* may have been St. Ambrose, as he and other early theologians struggled with making sense of why all of this happened.) Another important statement comes from Elder Orson F. Whitney:

> The fall had a wonderful two-fold direction—down-ward, yet forward. It brought man in the world and set his feet upon progression's highway. (*Saturday Night Thoughts* [1923], 93)

But let's back up for a minute, back to 2 Nephi 2:25. I appreciate that Lehi said to his son Jacob, "men are, that they might have joy," but notice the word *might*. I don't really know how much joy Jacob experienced. In fact, notice the apparent absence of joy in Jacob's closing words many years later:

> Our lives passed away like as it were unto us a dream, we being a lonesome and a solemn people, wanderers,

cast out from Jerusalem, born in tribulation, in a wilderness, and hated of our brethren, which caused wars
and contentions; wherefore, we did mourn out our
days. (Jacob 7:26)

No "happily ever after" there. Earth life is a tough
neighborhood. You might have joy, and then again, you
might not. Notice that among the inalienable rights mentioned in the American Declaration of Independence are
"life, liberty, and the *pursuit* of happiness." A *guarantee* of
happiness is not there. In other words, you might find happiness, and you might not, but you will have the right to
pursue it. Good luck to all of us on that.

On one particularly hard day when I was a teenager,
my dad said to me, "This too shall pass." On another day,
when everything was going great, Dad said again the same
words, "This too shall pass." Another way of expressing the
idea of "opposition in all things" is to say that we'll all have
ups and downs. I like to temper the potential joy mentioned in 2 Nephi 2:25 with a similar-sounding verse in
Moses 6:48. Enoch said:

> Because that Adam fell, we are; and by his fall came
> death; and we are made partakers of misery and woe.

Sometimes we have 2 Nephi 2:25 "joy" days, and sometimes we have Moses 6:48 "misery and woe" days. That is
all part of the experience of opposition in all things, and it
makes life painfully and wonderfully interesting. Or, to put
it another way, unfortunate events are part of the fortunate
fall.

Even the beatitudes in Matthew 5 and 3 Nephi 12 illustrate the "blessedness" of having opposition in all things. "Blessed are the poor in spirit," Jesus began, "for theirs is the kingdom of heaven." In the beatitudes, "Jesus turns ordinary ideas about happiness upside down" (*The Lion Handbook to the Bible*, ed. Pat Alexander and David Alexander [1973], 555). We would normally think the "blessed" are the rich in spirit, those who rejoice, those who are well off and independent, those who are self-sufficient, and so forth. But the Savior illustrates that opposition leads to blessedness when we come to him with our difficulties.

So while some may refer to Adam and Eve as the original idiots, our Bible Dictionary takes an opposite tone:

> The aggregate of the scriptures certifies that his transgression in the garden of Eden, although designated as a "fall," was necessary to the advancement and spiritual progress of humanity on this earth, and Adam rightly should be honored, not denigrated. Adam is the Ancient of Days and is also known as Michael. He is the archangel and will come again to the earth in power and glory as the patriarch of the human family preparatory to the Second Coming of Jesus Christ. (Bible Dictionary, "Adam," 604)

And what about Mother Eve? Was she the "devil's gateway" and a negative counterpart to Mary, as the earlier source suggested? No. President Joseph Fielding Smith commented:

One of these days, if I ever get to where I can speak to Mother Eve, I want to thank her for tempting Adam to partake of the fruit. He accepted the temptation, with the result that children came into this world. And when I kneel in prayer, I feel to thank Mother Eve, for if she had not had that influence over Adam, and if Adam had done according to the commandment first given to him, they would still be in the Garden of Eden and we would not be here at all. (*Seek Ye Earnestly* [1970], 4)

"So, Brother Bytheway," one student asked, "if it's all so positive, should we be calling it a fall at all?" Yeah, we probably should. I like to tell my class, "Raise your hand if you are responsible for the Fall of Adam." No hands go up. They understand that "men will be punished for their own sins, and not for Adam's transgression" (Articles of Faith 1:2). Then I say, "Raise your hand if you've been affected by the Fall of Adam," and all hands go up. Yes, we've inherited mortality, and we will eventually die. But we did not inherit Adam's sin. We learned how to sin on our own, all by ourselves. Elder Gerald N. Lund referred to these two events as the "fall of man" and the "fall of me."

As [Lehi] said, "Men are instructed sufficiently that they know good from evil." (2 Ne. 2:5.) If we know good from evil and then sin (which, according to Paul, all men do), then we must talk about a second fall. This is not the fall of Adam. This is *one's own personal fall.* This fall, which our own, not Adam's, transgression brings about, requires redemption as surely as mankind needed redemption from the consequences of Adam's fall. We'll term this the "fall of me." (*Jesus Christ: Key to the Plan of Salvation* [1991], 95; emphasis in original)

How can we be mad at Adam and Eve for falling just like we have?

So here we are, on a fallen earth, having inherited mortal bodies, including every kind of sickness or malady of body and mind, and we'll all end up dead. Is that all there is? (Sorry, rhetorical question.) Of course not! The Fall of Adam, we might say, is the sickness, and the Atonement of Jesus Christ is the cure (and more).

Chapter Five

THE NO-GAPS ATONEMENT OF JESUS CHRIST

I enjoy immensely hearing the experiences of my students, many of whom are returned missionaries. "When I was on *my* mission," I tell them (and this was a long time ago, mind you—Wilford Woodruff and I were companions), "there was no internet, no email, and no weekly phone calls. Letters from home took two weeks to arrive, so *any* bit of mail was an event."

Up until my mission, the arrival of the latest *Ensign* magazine at my home didn't generate that much excitement for me, but in the Philippines it did. I remember very clearly reading an article by Elder Bruce R. McConkie, "Christ and the Creation," in the June 1982 *Ensign*. Elder McConkie used a phrase in that article that I never forgot (little did I know that I'd be writing a chapter about it one day): the "three pillars of eternity." When I was a teenager, whenever Elder McConkie approached the pulpit in general conference, my dad would say, "Sit up straight, here it comes." So as I read his words as a missionary, it was easy to imagine his strong voice in my mind:

These three are the very pillars of eternity itself. They are the most important events that ever have or will occur in all eternity. They are the Creation, the Fall, and the Atonement.

As a nineteen-year-old, I didn't grasp the significance of the three pillars, but as I studied the Book of Mormon, I began to see those pillars, those "most important events," almost everywhere. More important, I began to see them as a chain of events—connected events, as the Book of Mormon does. In fact, I have seen visual aids created for the seminary system that depict a bridge representing our eternal journey supported by those three pillars.

We've already talked about the fortunate fall, and now we can ask, what does the Book of Mormon teach us about the Atonement of Jesus Christ?

"JESUS OF THE GAPS"

I was compelled to search my Book of Mormon for a better understanding of Christ's Atonement from an unlikely source—an evangelical minister.

I was seated in an airplane waiting to fly home to Utah from Newark, New Jersey, when a man sporting a "Vote for Pedro" T-shirt came walking down the aisle. I thought, "Oh, he's seen *Napoleon Dynamite*." He took the seat across the aisle, and, noticing that my wife and I were a little overdressed, he said, "Hi, guys, what were you doing up here?"

I said, "Oh, I gave a presentation to some missionaries in my church."

THE NO-GAPS ATONEMENT OF JESUS CHRIST   39

He said, "Really? That's what I'm doing here!" His name was Bryan, and he was a Free Evangelical Church minister.

As we started talking, I noticed a book in his carry-on called *A Different Jesus?* by Robert L. Millet. Dr. Millet, a Latter-day Saint scholar and author and former dean of Religious Education at BYU, wrote that book to address those who say, "Well, you Mormons say you believe in Jesus, but it's a different Jesus." I saw the book in Bryan's bag and said, "I know him! In fact, he was one of my professors." I asked him if he had ever seen the TV show featuring Robert Millet and Greg Johnson, an evangelical minister, who sit together and talk about their common and contrasting beliefs in a respectful way. It used to air on a local television station, and it was called *A Mormon and an Evangelical in Conversation.* "Have you ever seen that show?" I asked.

"Yeah," he said. "In fact, I know Greg."

Finally, I suggested, "Why don't we do that? Let's talk about what we believe and what's important to us. Let's have the Bryan and John show."

He said, "Okay," so we began talking. We had a friendly, open discussion about our doctrinal similarities and differences.

One of the first things he said to me was, "You guys believe in the Jesus of the gaps." Now, I have to confess I have a strange mind. I immediately pictured the Gap, the popular clothing store in the mall, and I thought to myself, "I really don't know where Jesus shopped." (I'm glad that thought didn't come out of my mouth.) He continued, "You guys think that you do this much, you do all this work, and then Jesus will make up the gap, or make up the difference in the end."

His point began to sink in. He was suggesting that we as Latter-day Saints minimize the Atonement of Christ by thinking that we do part or most of the saving work ourselves. To paraphrase Bryan, "You guys believe in the Jesus of the gaps, and that is a different Jesus. Therefore you don't qualify as a Christian." He didn't say it that strongly, but I knew what he meant. The idea that we minimize the Atonement of Christ was offensive to him, and, to be honest, it was offensive to me as well.

As I pondered it, I could see how others might think we are taking Jesus out of the equation, or at least minimizing his role. We sometimes even use phrases that promote that idea: "If you'll just do everything you can, the Lord will make up the rest," or "Do your part, do your best, then let go and let God do the rest," or "Work as if everything depends on you, pray as if everything depends on God, and God will fill in the gap." Perhaps we take this "do your part" idea too far and begin to apply it to our salvation, where it really doesn't belong.

Remember the three pillars of eternity? Do we cross this bridge to eternal life mostly by ourselves, and then Jesus bridges any gap that our efforts didn't cover? Where might we get this idea? One of the main places might be from this oft-quoted verse from Nephi:

> We labor diligently to write, to persuade our children, and also our brethren, to believe in Christ, and

to be reconciled to God; for we know that it is by grace
that we are saved, after all we can do. (2 Nephi 25:23)

The last phrase in that verse, "after all we can do," is, I
believe, where much confusion can begin. Sometimes we
might erroneously look at the grace of Christ as part of
a formula with a set sequence—I have to do all this, and
then finally, at the end, my scores are added up, grace kicks
in, and Jesus fills in the gap.

Bryan and I talked about lots of things on that flight,
and that night I had trouble sleeping as I recalled my answers. But that "Jesus of the gaps" question made my stom-
ach ache. I couldn't get it off my mind. I knew that the last
thing we would want to do is minimize the Atonement of
Jesus Christ. I knew that the idea of "the gap" was offensive, as it should be. So I went to work.

Here was my question—do we really earn or "merit" our
own salvation, much like I would earn an Eagle Scout award
by my hard work and accumulation of the required "merit"
badges? I opened the index of my triple combination and
looked for references under the word *merit*. I found seven
scriptures and determined that I would locate this so-called
"gap." Here was the big question: *How much do we do, and
how much does the Lord do when it comes to our salvation?
How big or how small is this gap? Or does any gap exist at all?*

A quick screenshot of the merit references from the
index to the triple combination gives us a rapid education
regarding "the gap." The law of witnesses says "in the mouths
of two or three . . ." but here we have seven witnesses, all different authors, the last being the Savior himself!

Merit

See also Grace; Jesus Christ, Atonement through; Mercy; Virtue;
  Worth

no flesh can dwell in God's presence, save through *merits* of the
  Messiah, 2 Ne. 2:8.
rely wholly upon *merits* of him who is mighty to save, 2 Ne.
  31:19.
since man had fallen, he could not *merit* anything of himself,
  Alma 22:14.
God has taken away guilt from hearts through *merits* of his Son,
  Alma 24:10.
have remission of sins through Christ's *merits*, Hel. 14:13.
rely alone upon *merits* of Christ, Moro. 6:4.

rely upon *merits* of Christ, D&C 3:20.

Now, shall we go into more depth? *Surely in these seven
verses we will discover the size of this so-called gap!* The first
reference is from Lehi talking to his son Jacob:

> 2 Nephi 2:8: Wherefore, how great the importance
> to make these things known unto the inhabitants of the
> earth, that they may know that there is no flesh that
> can dwell in the presence of God, save it be through the
> merits, and mercy, and grace of the Holy Messiah.

The merits spoken of in this verse are not our merits,
but the merits of Christ. Jacob was born in the wilderness.
He never saw Jerusalem, and he grew up in an environ-
ment of constant family conflict. He needed to understand
the role of opposition in our mortal existence, but he also
needed hope in Christ and hope for a better world.

So that's the first reference to merits. It is not exactly
clear from that verse what Jesus does and what we do, so

let's keep looking. Our next reference to *merits* comes from Nephi:

> 2 Nephi 31:19: And now, my beloved brethren, after ye have gotten into this strait and narrow path, I would ask if all is done? Behold, I say unto you, Nay; for ye have not come thus far save it were by the word of Christ with unshaken faith in him, relying wholly upon the merits of him who is mighty to save.

That's a little stronger, isn't it? Once again, any merits of our own are not mentioned. Nephi declares that we must rely "wholly" upon the merits of Christ, who is "mighty to save."

Well, two down, five to go. Our next reference to *merits* comes from Aaron, the brother of Ammon, teaching King Lamoni's father:

> Alma 22:14: And since man had fallen he could not merit anything of himself; but the sufferings and death of Christ atone for their sins, through faith and repentance, and so forth.

For me, this little scriptural search began to be more fascinating than I thought it would be. We can't earn *any* merits? Apparently not. Aaron says that man cannot merit *anything* of himself.

But we're not even halfway through! It gets more interesting. Our next reference was spoken by Anti-Nephi-Lehi, the leader of the converted Lamanites:

> Alma 24:10: I also thank my God, yea, my great God, that he hath granted unto us that we might repent

of these things, and also that he hath forgiven us of those our many sins and murders which we have committed, and taken away the guilt from our hearts, through the merits of his Son.

Are we seeing a pattern here? The consistent message is that it is not through our own merits but through the merits of the Son of God that our guilt is taken away.

This is getting more and more interesting, isn't it? We have three more. Here is Samuel the Lamanite's testimony:

> Helaman 14:12–13: And also that ye might know of the coming of Jesus Christ, the Son of God, the Father of heaven and of earth, the Creator of all things from the beginning; and that ye might know of the signs of his coming, to the intent that ye might believe on his name. And if ye believe on his name ye will repent of all your sins, that thereby ye may have a remission of them through his merits.

Once again, it is the merits of Christ that bring a remission of our sins, enabling us to dwell with God one day.

There are two more references to *merits* left in the index. The next verse is from Moroni, in one of the closing chapters of the Book of Mormon:

> Moroni 6:4: And after they had been received unto baptism, and were wrought upon and cleansed by the power of the Holy Ghost, they were numbered among the people of the church of Christ; and their names were taken, that they might be remembered and nourished by the good word of God, to keep them in the right way, to keep them continually watchful unto

prayer, relying alone upon the merits of Christ, who was the author and the finisher of their faith.

From Nephi to Moroni, from a prophet in 600 BC to another in AD 400, the message over a thousand years is the same. Nephi says we should rely "wholly" and Moroni says we rely "alone" upon the merits of Christ.

The last *merits* reference comes from a revelation of Jesus Christ himself regarding the purposes of the Book of Mormon:

> D&C 3:19–20: And for this very purpose are these plates preserved, which contain these records—that the promises of the Lord might be fulfilled, which he made to his people; and that the Lamanites might come to the knowledge of their fathers, and that they might know the promises of the Lord, and that they may believe the gospel and rely upon the merits of Jesus Christ, and be glorified through faith in his name, and that through their repentance they might be saved. Amen.

Let's review how we did on our assignment. Did we find the gap? From what we've read, how much do we do, and how much does Jesus Christ do? I couldn't find a gap in there, could you? I only wish I had memorized these verses before I had met Bryan, my evangelical minister friend on the plane. The inescapable conclusion is that we cannot "merit anything" of ourselves, and we must rely "wholly" and "alone" upon Christ and his merits.

When we reviewed these verses in one of my Book of Mormon classes, one of my students raised her hand and asked, "Are you saying that we cannot earn our salvation?" My response was, "That is exactly what these scriptures are saying." And there are other scriptures that teach this too. Didn't King Benjamin observe, "Are we not all beggars?" (Mosiah 4:19). Yes. We *all* are. None of us can tell the Lord, "I don't need to beg for my salvation. I earned it—I merited it!" Nope, can't be done. Jesus did for us what we could not do for ourselves.

I suggest that the whole idea of the "gap" comes largely from a misunderstanding or misinterpretation of the phrase "after all we can do" in 2 Nephi 25:23. Brother Brad Wilcox has written an excellent book on this subject, *The Continuous Atonement,* the title itself implying that the Savior's Atonement is not waiting to take effect "after" all we can do, but that the grace of Christ is immediate and continuous. Elder Bruce C. Hafen has also spoken about this idea:

> The Savior's gift of grace to us is not necessarily limited in time to "after" all we can do. We may receive his grace before, during, and after the time when we expend our own efforts. (*The Broken Heart* [1989], 155–56)

Another interesting way we can look at the phrase "after all we can we do" is to focus on the word *we*. Repeat the phrase to yourself emphasizing just that word: What can *we* do? Just we, by ourselves? Perhaps we could let the Book of Mormon itself answer.

WHAT CAN *WE* DO? ANYTHING?

Earlier, we read of the words of Anti-Nephi-Lehi in Alma 24:10, who testified that his guilt was taken away through the merits of Christ. In the very next verse, he actually uses a phrase—twice—that is very similar to "after all we can do." It's almost as if he is answering the question, "What can we do?"

> And now behold, my brethren, since it has been *all that we could do* (as we were the most lost of all mankind) to repent of all our sins and the many murders which we have committed, and to get God to take them away from our hearts, for it was *all we could do* to repent sufficiently before God that he would take away our stain. (Alma 24:11; emphasis added)

In other words, by this usage, "all we can do" is:

1. Exercise faith in Christ
2. Repent

And already, we've come to the end of our list. Can we be baptized by ourselves? No, we need Jesus's Church. We need his priesthood. We need an authorized servant. So we can't do that. Can we, by ourselves, receive the gift of the Holy Ghost? No. Again, we need his Church, and we need his authorized servants. Can we, by ourselves, receive any other ordinances? No, we need Jesus Christ, his gospel, and his authorized servants. And since faith "must be centered in Jesus Christ" (Bible Dictionary, "Faith," 669), and repentance is made possible by the Atonement of Jesus Christ, we need him even for those first steps!

So we may ask again, where is the gap? It seems to me that there is no gap, and that on our own, we get nowhere. We don't even get started. We really must rely on Christ, who was described by Moroni as the "author *and* the finisher" of our faith (Moroni 6:4; emphasis added; see also Hebrews 12:2). Not merely the finisher, who is there at the end to fill in the gap, but the author, who walks alongside us from the very beginning. C. S. Lewis observed:

> After the first few steps in the Christian life we realise that everything which really needs to be done in our souls can be done only by God. (*Mere Christianity* [Macmillan, 1960], 150)

Speaking of what we can do, Jesus himself taught:

> I am the vine, ye are the branches: He that abideth in me, and I in him, the same bringeth forth much fruit: for *without me ye can do nothing*. (John 15:5; emphasis added)

WHAT IS THE PLACE OF GOOD WORKS, THEN?

So, Brother Bytheway, if we cannot do anything, why does Nephi use that phrase, "after all we can do"? One way to think of it is this—*after all we can do, it will never be enough*. We are saved by the grace of Christ. That doesn't mean we shouldn't strive to be better people. I love the word *strive* and the idea of striving. We *can* do good works, and we should! The issue is about salvation and its relationship to our works. We are in error if we think we can merit our salvation or earn our way to heaven through our works. The scriptures clearly testify that we cannot.

And yet, good works are clearly part of our theology, and they are also mentioned throughout the scriptural record. Alma taught that "the day cometh that all shall rise from the dead and stand before God, and be judged according to their works" (Alma 11:41; see also 2 Nephi 28:23; Revelation 20:12, 13). I love the statement of C. S. Lewis:

> Christians have often disputed as to whether what leads the Christian home is good actions, or Faith in Christ. I have no right really to speak on such a difficult question, but it does seem to me like asking which blade in a pair of scissors is most necessary. (*Mere Christianity,* 115)

It is my belief that good works will flow more naturally from a changed heart. In other words, good works are the fruits, the natural result, and the evidence of being born again. Good works are a fruit of salvation, not a formula for salvation. Or, to paraphrase Moroni, good works are necessary but not sufficient—only the grace of Christ is sufficient for salvation (see Moroni 10:32).

"So perhaps," some might conclude, "I shouldn't do anything, any ministering, any service, any fulfilling of welfare assignments, until my heart is changed and my motives are entirely pure." Well, if that were the case, nothing would ever get done. We can't stagnate waiting for only the purest motives before we will move.

COME TO CHRIST TO BECOME LIKE CHRIST

Then why are we working so hard? The question is one of intent: Are we doing the work to try to save ourselves? Are we working hard, doing all the things we are asked to do, so that we can "make it" to the celestial kingdom? No.

We are doing the work because the work of the gospel helps us become the kind of people the Lord wants us to become. The question we must ask ourselves as we go through life choosing how to spend our time is not "What am I thinking here?" or "What am I doing here?" but "What am I becoming here?" Good works are part of the process of becoming.

When Sister Naomi Randall wrote "I Am a Child of God," her original lyrics were, "Teach me all that I must know to live with Him someday." President Spencer W. Kimball suggested that it be changed to "teach me all that I must *do* . . ." In October 2000, then-Elder Dallin H. Oaks gave a talk in general conference titled "The Challenge to Become." *Become* is a wonderful word.

Knowing what to do is nice. Doing what we know is even better. But becoming what we are to become is the ultimate goal. I have no right to suggest such a thing, but in light of President Oaks's address, I would love it if the song were changed once again to say, "teach me all that I must *be* . . ." which involves knowing what to do, doing what we know, and, with the Savior's grace, becoming what the Lord wants us to become. As my friend Brad Wilcox says, "We are not earning heaven, but learning heaven" by striving to become the type of beings who would be comfortable there.

In other words, we have come *to* Christ, and now we are trying to become *like* Christ—which, we must add, is impossible to accomplish without Christ! He accompanies us on our journey to become *like* him through our covenants. Jesus himself taught, "What manner of men ought ye to be? . . . even as I am" (3 Nephi 27: 27). We've "Come unto Jesus," as one song says, and now we're "Trying to Be like Jesus," as another song says. I have my own version, "I'm failing to be like Jesus . . . ," which I sing to myself when I'm faced with my imperfections. However, in such moments Nephi has taught me to say, "Nevertheless, I know in whom I have trusted. My God hath been my support" (2 Nephi 4:19–20).

If there is a chasm to be crossed starting from where we begin and ending at where we want to be, the Savior and his grace, or his "enabling power," are there from the very beginning to the very end. I simply cannot find a gap or a place where the Savior is not there.

INFINITE IN SCOPE

Not only does the Book of Mormon teach about the Atonement of Jesus Christ, but it tells us that his Atonement is infinite. (How can there be a gap in something that is infinite?) Amulek, in teaching the people that animal sacrifices under the law of Moses would eventually end with a "last sacrifice," testified:

> For it is expedient that there should be a great and last sacrifice; yea, not a sacrifice of man, neither of beast, neither of any manner of fowl; for it shall not be a human sacrifice; but it must be an infinite and eternal sacrifice. (Alma 34:10)

This last sacrifice would be the Son of God, or the "Lamb of God," as John the Baptist called him (see John 1:29). It would be the sacrifice of a divine being, thus, not a human sacrifice. In what other ways is the Atonement of Jesus Christ infinite? President Russell M. Nelson answered:

> In preparatory times of the Old Testament, the prac-
> tice of atonement was finite—meaning it had an end.
> It was a symbolic forecast of the definitive Atonement
> of Jesus the Christ. His Atonement is infinite—without
> an end [see 2 Nephi 9:7; 25:16; Alma 34:10, 12, 14]. It
> was also infinite in that all humankind would be saved
> from never-ending death. It was infinite in terms of
> His immense suffering. It was infinite in time, putting
> an end to the preceding prototype of animal sacrifice.
> It was infinite in scope—it was to be done once for all
> [see Hebrews 10:10]. And the mercy of the Atonement
> extends not only to an infinite number of people, but
> also to an infinite number of worlds created by Him [see
> D&C 76:24; Moses 1:33]. It was infinite beyond any
> human scale of measurement or mortal comprehension.
> ("The Atonement," *Ensign*, November 1996)

Some in the Christian world have wrestled with what will happen to those who have lived and died having never heard about Christ, without a chance to repent and be baptized during their time on earth. What will happen to them? King Benjamin addressed the infinite scope of Christ's Atonement when he taught, so briefly and concisely:

> For behold, and also his blood atoneth for the sins
> of those who have fallen by the transgression of Adam,
> who have died not knowing the will of God concerning
> them, or who have ignorantly sinned. (Mosiah 3:11)

Wow, what a verse! Slow down a little, read it again, and consider how these doctrinal points are a refreshing and relieving drink of living water, especially when we consider how many of our brothers and sisters have lived on this earth without a knowledge of God.

Additionally, Jesus was the only one who could offer such an infinite Atonement, since he was born of a mortal mother and an immortal Father. Because of that unique birthright, Jesus was an infinite being.

The Book of Mormon testifies that the Savior died not only for our sins, but for a range of problems, pains, and afflictions experienced in this earth life (see Alma 7:11–12).

JUSTICE, MERCY, AND THE ATONEMENT

How does a God who is perfectly merciful demand justice? And how can a God of perfect justice extend mercy so freely?

Some of my students find this confusing, especially when they hear things from their friends like, "Well, I think God is love, and I think he is just so loving and forgiving that in the end he'll let a lot of things go and say 'never mind' to all that punishment stuff." In their minds, this makes God more loving and more merciful. However, it would also make him unjust. How can God be a God of justice and a God of mercy at the same time? How can he balance love and law?

Thankfully, the Book of Mormon explains beautifully how "justice, love, and mercy meet" ("How Great the Wisdom and the Love," *Hymns* [1985], no. 195), and how justice and mercy can both be satisfied through a mediator, or someone who will meet the demands of justice while extending mercy to us.

Those who know me know that I love to talk about my dad and his incredible World War II experiences. On February 21, 1945, two days before the marines hoisted the Stars and Stripes at Iwo Jima, the aircraft carrier *USS Saratoga* (CV-3), while on patrol northwest of that island, was attacked by kamikazes. My father, just a teenager at the time, stayed at his post on a quad 40mm antiaircraft gun and fought for his life and the lives of his shipmates. Soon after the attack began, he reported:

> I glanced out over the water, and I saw one of our de-stroyers coming across our bow at flank speed and firing every gun it had. Apparently, the attacking aircraft were coming in from our starboard bow, and the destroyers were moving into position to protect our bow. ("Jack Bytheway Autobiography," unpublished manuscript)

As I imagine this scene, I marvel at the gallantry, the bravery, and the sacrifice displayed by the commanders of these destroyers. They were saying to the enemy, "If you're going to attack the carrier, you're going to have to go through us. *We will stand between you and them.*"

When I envision that selfless, protective action, I am reminded of the beautiful words of Abinadi, who spoke of our loving Savior "standing betwixt [us] and justice; having . . . taken upon himself [our] iniquity and [our] transgres-sions, having redeemed [us], and satisfied the demands of justice" (Mosiah 15:9).

I marvel at the gallantry, the bravery, the sacrifice, and the love of our Savior, willingly standing between us and justice! Notice, the need for justice wasn't discarded because of his divine love for us; the demands of justice still had to be satisfied. Jesus willingly took the brunt, satisfied justice, then turned and extended mercy to us. Alma explained:

> Therefore God himself atoneth for the sins of the world, to bring about the plan of mercy, to appease the demands of justice, that God might be a perfect, just God, and a merciful God also. (Alma 42:15)

Alma continued, "Justice exerciseth all his demands, and also mercy claimeth all which is her own" (Alma 42:24). (Interesting that justice is characterized as a male and mercy as a female, isn't it?)

Evidently, Alma's son Corianton thought it was "unjust" that God could condemn sinners to a state of misery. As mentioned above, my students hear similar arguments today: "I don't think it's right for God to do that; that's not fair. I just can't believe a God of love would send sinners to hell." I believe Corianton's concerns were preserved because those who compiled the Book of Mormon saw our day.

In addition, I believe that there was more behind Corianton's objection than just a doctrinal misunderstanding. I believe Alma was granted some discernment concerning his son's problems. Near the end of Alma 42, Alma gave us another clue about why Corianton might have been trying to explain away the justice of God:

> Do not endeavor to excuse yourself in the least point
> because of your sins, by denying the justice of God. . . .
> (v. 30)

It sounds as if Corianton was looking for a way to excuse his behavior. If we believe God isn't harmonizing the justice vs. mercy thing to our satisfaction, perhaps we think it's okay for us to do whatever we want. That way we can excuse our own sins. Alma says "not so":

> And now, my son, I desire that ye should let these
> things trouble you no more, and only let your sins
> trouble you, with that trouble which shall bring you
> down unto repentance. (Alma 42:29)

In other words, Son, you're worried about the wrong things. Alma's advice could be easily applied in our day: Stop worrying about the doctrine and policies you don't understand, and get your own act together. *Only let your sins trouble you*—that should be your main concern!

Certainly we are allowed to grapple with doctrine and policies—wrestle, ponder, and pray all you can. But our main concern, our top priority, should be seeking mercy and forgiveness for our own sins. In that repentant posture, we find our Savior standing ready to mercifully satisfy the demands of justice for us.

Why do we need the Book of Mormon? The intertwining, balancing, and harmonizing of justice and mercy are beautifully explained by Abinadi to King Noah and the wicked priests (Mosiah 15), by Amulek to the Zoramites (Alma 34), and by Alma to his son Corianton (Alma 42).

Obviously, so much more could be said about the Atonement of Jesus Christ, so many more aspects of the Atonement explored, and so many more books will be written in gratitude to the Lord Jesus Christ for his infinite loving sacrifice. Forgive me if I didn't cover your favorite part in this chapter.

As for me, I'm thankful to my Father in Heaven for Bryan (the evangelical minister I met on the plane), for the Book of Mormon, and for the bridge supported by the three pillars of eternity— the Creation, the Fall, and the Atonement—all part of our Father's plan made possible by Jesus Christ, who stood "betwixt us and justice," giving his own life so that we might have eternal life.

Chapter Six

I'M BAPTIZED, BUT AM I BORN AGAIN?

One day I began class by asking, "Are 'baptism' and being 'born again' the same thing? Are they just different words that have the same meaning?"

Some nodded "yes," but rather tentatively, while others shook their heads in a "No, I don't think so . . ." gesture while carefully watching my expression for a hint. What do you think? We have often heard baptism compared to our being born again, since in both experiences one is surrounded by or immersed in water and then comes forth. But are they really the same thing? Consider these Book of Mormon verses, and watch for the very strong word *must* in each of them. (I'll *italicize* it so you don't miss it.)

Mosiah 27:25: Marvel not that all mankind, yea, men and women, all nations, kindreds, tongues and people, *must* be born again.

Alma 5:49: I say unto you the aged, and also the middle aged, and the rising generation; yea, to cry unto them that they *must* repent and be born again.

Alma 7:14: Now I say unto you that ye *must* repent,

and be born again; for the Spirit saith if ye are not born again ye cannot inherit the kingdom of heaven.

Here are a couple of references from outside the Book of Mormon:

> Moses 6:59: Even so ye *must* be born again into the kingdom of heaven, of water, and of the Spirit, and be cleansed by blood, even the blood of mine Only Begotten.

> John 3:7: Marvel not that I said unto thee, Ye *must* be born again.

If being born again is an absolute *must,* then we absolutely *must* know what it means, wouldn't you say? If we ask the same question another way, the answer becomes a little more clear. I can point to the exact date when I was baptized. I have the certificate somewhere. Can I point to the exact date when I was "born again"? That sounds a little different, doesn't it? Consider the question Alma asked the Saints in Zarahemla:

> Alma 5:14: And now behold, I ask of you, my brethren of the church, have ye spiritually been born of God? Have ye received his image in your countenances? Have ye experienced this mighty change in your hearts?

There's our answer—"my brethren *of the church*" (they've been baptized), "have ye spiritually been *born of God*?" Alma appears to be asking baptized members of the Church if they've been born again! So, obviously, being baptized and being born again are not the same thing.

I like to think of it this way: baptism is an event, while being born again is a process. Perhaps we could even say that baptism is a part of the process of being born again. Elder David A. Bednar explained:

> We begin the process of being born again through exercising faith in Christ, repenting of our sins, and being baptized by immersion for the remission of sins by one having priesthood authority. . . . After we come out of the waters of baptism, our souls need to be continuously immersed in and saturated with the truth and the light of the Savior's gospel. Sporadic and shallow dipping in the doctrine of Christ and partial participation in His restored Church cannot produce the spiritual transformation that enables us to walk in a newness of life. Rather, fidelity to covenants, constancy of commitment, and offering our whole soul unto God are required if we are to receive the blessings of eternity. . . . Total immersion in and saturation with the Savior's gospel are essential steps in the process of being born again. ("Ye Must Be Born Again," *Ensign,* May 2007)

Since baptism is an event and being born again is a process, we might compare them to a temple wedding and a celestial marriage. It might be easy to get the two confused at first, but a temple wedding is an event, whereas achieving a celestial marriage is a lifelong endeavor. One is a beginning, and the other is a "becoming."

THE EVENT OF BAPTISM

Okay, what about baptism, then? What is uniquely taught in the Book of Mormon about the event of baptism? Time for another screenshot (widely used by my Gen Z students, who carry many of their books on their phones).

Right away we see something interesting. *Baptism* is mentioned only once in the Old Testament (and not in the actual text, but in a chapter synopsis). *Baptism* appears twenty-seven times in the New Testament and thirty-two times in the Book of Mormon.

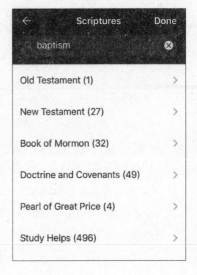

Why is baptism never mentioned in the Old Testament? For one thing, it is a Greek word, and the Old Testament was written in Hebrew. Was Jesus the first to be baptized? Well, we know that John the Baptist was baptizing *before* Jesus and John the Baptist met, so the answer is no. Exactly when did baptism start? In our understanding, baptism has always been around.

The Bible Dictionary explains:

> Baptism has always been practiced whenever the gospel of Jesus Christ has been on the earth and has been taught by men holding the holy priesthood who could administer the ordinances. Although there is some obscurity in the Bible as to the antiquity of baptism

before the time of Jesus, from latter-day revelation it is
clear that Adam was baptized (Moses 6:64–68) and that
the patriarchs and prophets since his time have taught
the gospel and administered the ordinances that pertain
to the gospel. (Bible Dictionary, "Baptism," 618)

In the Bible, we have John the Baptist performing bap-
tisms (which evidently wasn't so unusual, since the Jews
had for a long time participated in ritual baths and wash-
ings like the *mikveh*).

Those who questioned John the Baptist were not so concerned about what he was doing; they were questioning who
he was, or who he claimed to be. The Book of Mormon provides wonderful clarity about baptism having been a part of
the gospel since Adam, clarity lost from the Bible since baptism is mentioned only in the New Testament. By contrast,
Book of Mormon prophets taught baptism long before Jesus
was born. As early as 2 Nephi, Nephi taught about baptism,
comparing it to a gate to the path back to God:

> For the gate by which ye should enter is repentance
> and baptism by water; and then cometh a remission of
> your sins by fire and by the Holy Ghost. (2 Nephi 31:17)

Once again, the gate is like an event, and the path beyond the gate is a process, or a way of life.

We know from the Bible that baptism is important because Jesus was baptized, and after his Resurrection he told
the Apostles, "Go ye therefore, and teach all nations, baptizing them in the name of the Father, and of the Son, and
of the Holy Ghost" (Matthew 28:19).

What covenant are we making at baptism? Beyond the born-again symbolism, what are we agreeing to do? We have a great answer from the Book of Mormon. After Alma the Elder defended Abinadi and escaped with his life, he came back into town and beckoned those who believed Abinadi to follow him to the Waters of Mormon. There, at the water's edge, Alma asked the people if they would be willing to be baptized, and he gave them a nice explanation of what their baptism meant. Elder Jeffrey R. Holland explained:

> These new disciples would also demonstrate their faith by:
> - Coming into the fold of God.
> - Being called his people.
> - Bearing one another's burdens.
> - Mourning with those that mourn.
> - Comforting those who stand in need of comfort.
> - Standing as witnesses of God at all times and in all things and in all places.
> - Entering into a covenant to serve God and keep his commandments.
>
> This declaration by Alma at the Waters of Mormon still stands as the most complete scriptural statement on record as to what the newly baptized commit to do and be. (*Christ and the New Covenant* [1997], 106)

As you look over that list, isn't it interesting how much of the baptismal covenant involves ministering to others? Of course, baptism is a very individual decision and event, but the baptismal covenant makes us part of a community that covenants to care about one another.

Toward the close of the Book of Mormon record, Moroni shares a letter he received from his father, Mormon, who began, "If I have learned the truth, there have been disputations among you concerning the baptism of your little children" (Moroni 8:5). Indeed, and there continue to be disputations today about the purpose, mode, and necessity of baptism.

Mormon declares that repentance and baptism are available for "those who are accountable and capable of committing sin" (Moroni 8:10), which means baptism is a choice each individual makes when he or she is old enough to comprehend right and wrong and make such a choice.

Once again, we see the clarifying role of the Book of Mormon.

THE PROCESS OF BEING BORN AGAIN

Once the event of baptism is behind us, what do we do next? We have passed through the gate, to use Nephi's words, and now we continue, or we "press forward" down the path of being born again. Nephi seemed to anticipate that very question:

> And now, my beloved brethren, after ye have gotten into this strait and narrow path, I would ask if all is done? Behold, I say unto you, Nay; for ye have not come thus far save it were by the word of Christ with unshaken faith in him, relying wholly upon the merits of him who is mighty to save. (2 Nephi 31:19)

And Nephi also gave the answer, along with a promise:

> Ye must press forward with a steadfastness in Christ,
> having a perfect brightness of hope, and a love of God
> and of all men. Wherefore, if ye shall press forward,
> feasting upon the word of Christ, and endure to the
> end, behold, thus saith the Father: Ye shall have eternal
> life. (2 Nephi 31:20)

The word *forward* requires some clarification, as it can
mean a variety of things in different circumstances. For
instance, if I'm facing north and you're facing south, the
simple definition of *forward* for each of us is relative to
which way we are facing.

How can we know we are moving "forward"? Some
people may believe that everyone needs to find his or her
own "forward," whatever that might be. In their way of
thinking, something may be true for you but not true for
me. We call that "moral relativism." In other words, *forward* means whatever I want it to mean. It's relative.

But Nephi doesn't leave us any wiggle room. His definition of *forward* includes the phrases "with a steadfastness in Christ" and "feasting upon [his] word." The path
we are on has a direction, and that direction is toward
Christ. Forward is Christward. Any other direction is not
forward.

This forward path is a long one, but it is a wonderful
path. I don't know if we'll ever feel like we've "arrived."
Elder D. Todd Christofferson commented on the "born
again" path as a process, not a destination:

You may ask, Why doesn't this mighty change happen more quickly with me? You should remember that
the remarkable examples of King Benjamin's people,
Alma, and some others in scripture are just that—remarkable and not typical. For most of us, the changes
are more gradual and occur over time. Being born
again, unlike our physical birth, is more a process than
an event. And engaging in that process is the central
purpose of mortality. ("Born Again," *Ensign*, May 2008)

A word of caution about measuring our progress
along the path might be appropriate. When we read the
scriptures, we are often reading about fellow travelers on
this path whose experiences are exceptional, not typical.
Most of us would love to have an Enos experience, a King
Lamoni experience, or even a more frightening, "stop-you-
in-your-tracks" experience like the Apostle Paul, Alma the
Younger, or the four sons of Mosiah. Who wouldn't like
to see an angel? Even if it scared you a little at first? Sign
me up. However, without such a visitation, it might just
require a little more faith for us to keep plodding along
without anything really spectacular to report. To give an
additional witness to what Elder Christofferson said, let me
include the words of President Ezra Taft Benson:

But we must be cautious as we discuss these remarkable examples. Though they are real and powerful, they
are the exception more than the rule. For every Paul,
for every Enos, and for every King Lamoni, there are
hundreds and thousands of people who find the process of repentance much more subtle, much more

imperceptible. Day by day they move closer to the Lord, little realizing they are building a godlike life. They live quiet lives of goodness, service, and commitment. They are like the Lamanites, who the Lord said "were baptized with fire and with the Holy Ghost, and they knew it not." (3 Ne. 9:20.) ("A Mighty Change of Heart," *Ensign*, October 1989)

Have you ever heard the journalism expression, "If it bleeds, it leads"? Kind of a dismal thought, but it describes why some stories make it to the front page or to the top of the news site although they might be less typical or of lesser importance in the grand scheme of things. But if some random citizen pulled out a phone and got a photo or video of the event, and if it will lead to more clicks, it might just lead the news day.

Those who compiled the scriptures had purer motives than merely accumulating clicks, to be sure, but we might still ask the question: when it comes to the scriptures, are the experiences recorded there typical or remarkable? If I'm not having the type of experiences that people in the scriptures are having, am I less worthy? Elder Bruce R. McConkie gave an answer that I have appreciated immensely:

Being born again is a gradual thing, except in a few isolated instances that are so miraculous that they get written up in the scriptures. As far as the generality of the members of the Church are concerned, we are born again by degrees, and we are born again to added light and added knowledge and added desires for righteousness as

we keep the commandments. ("Jesus Christ and Him
Crucified," BYU Devotional, September 5, 1976)

Being born again is a line-upon-line, precept-upon-
precept experience. For most of us, it is almost imperceptible, which can be frustrating. Sometimes we wonder if
we are making any progress at all. To me, the very fact that
we are wondering is a sign that we *are* progressing—we are
concerned about whether we are coming to Christ, which
is a wonderful concern, and even coming slowly is becoming eventually.

POWER IN THE PROCESS BY PARTAKING

We often speak of Jesus "visiting the Nephites" after his
Resurrection, but that's not entirely accurate—there were
Lamanites there too:

> And it came to pass that in the ending of the thirty
> and fourth year, behold, I will show unto you that the
> people of Nephi who were spared, and also those who
> had been called Lamanites, who had been spared, did
> have great favors shown unto them, and great blessings
> poured out upon their heads, insomuch that soon after
> the ascension of Christ into heaven he did truly mani-
> fest himself unto them. (3 Nephi 10:18)

It would be more accurate to say he visited the righteous, regardless of their genealogy or affiliation. Jesus appeared in the land Bountiful as recorded in 3 Nephi 11,
and his teachings to the people are preserved in 3 Nephi
12 through 16. Then, at the beginning of 3 Nephi 17,
we read that he told them he had to leave. I don't know

what kind of time constraints the Savior of the world has, but his exact words were: "Behold, my time is at hand" and "now I go unto the Father" (3 Nephi 17:1, 4). At this point, the people "did look steadfastly upon him as if they would ask him to tarry a little longer with them" (v. 5).

I find it wonderful that, in answer to the unspoken desire of the people to have Jesus stay with them, he instituted the sacrament, which included the promise, "Ye shall have my Spirit to be with you" (3 Nephi 18:7). The timing is hard to miss. To paraphrase, "I cannot stay with you in person, but I have prepared a way that you can always have my Spirit to be with you."

It is interesting to note that before Jesus actually appeared in person, the voice of Jesus Christ spoke and announced, "Ye shall offer up unto me no more the shedding of blood" (3 Nephi 9:19). The fact that Jesus spoke this commandment before he even appeared lets us know of its importance. Every sacrifice prescribed by the law of Moses was a shadow of the great and last sacrifice who was Christ—no longer the Passover lamb, but the Lamb of God.

With that in mind, at the beginning of 3 Nephi 18, Jesus commanded his disciples to bring forth bread and wine, and after he had blessed it, he let them know that this simple practice of eating in remembrance of him should be continued:

> Behold there shall one be ordained among you, and
> to him will I give power that he shall break bread and
> bless it and give it unto the people of my church, unto

all those who shall believe and be baptized in my name.
(3 Nephi 18:5)

Today, in our sacrament meetings, those who hold
the Aaronic Priesthood have specific tasks in preparing,
blessing, and passing the sacrament. In the past, I have
wondered why the teachers place the bread in the trays,
but do not break it—that privilege is left for the priests.
The priests break the bread while we are singing a hymn
about Jesus Christ, and we place the priests in the front of
the chapel where all can see. Why? The Book of Mormon
helped answer this question for me. A closer reading of the
verse above shows that some are given power, not just to
bless, but "power that he shall *break* bread." So perhaps the
fact that the teachers prepare but only the priests break and
bless is a priesthood issue. Interesting!

The sacrament of the Lord's Supper, as taught in the
Book of Mormon, is not just a Christmas and Easter event,
but a weekly event! Jesus continued:

> And this shall ye *always observe to do,* even as I have
> done, even as I have broken bread and blessed it and
> given it unto you. And this shall ye do in remembrance
> of my body, which I have shown unto you. And it shall
> be a testimony unto the Father that ye do always re-
> member me. And if ye do always remember me ye shall
> have my Spirit to be with you. (3 Nephi 18:6–7; em-
> phasis added)

The practice of partaking of bread and wine was to
continue ever after. In the closing chapters of the Book

of Mormon, Moroni includes what I like to call a mini "Handbook of Instructions" in Moroni 6. Moroni mentions that the Church members "did meet together oft to partake of bread and wine, in remembrance of the Lord Jesus" (Moroni 6:6).

The sacrifices of the law of Moses were intended to help the children of Israel look forward to the great and last sacrifice, the Atonement of the Lamb of God, Jesus Christ. Today, we partake of the sacrament looking backward in remembrance to that very same night when his Atonement began. What a night that was! No wonder we call it the meridian of time!

That one night, the event of the Atonement of Jesus Christ, gives us power in the process of being born again. By always remembering him, we can always have with us the Spirit that makes the process effective. The Book of Mormon shows how baptism, the sacrament, and being born again are all related in a continuous process of growth and conversion.

Chapter Seven

WHAT HAPPENS AFTER DEATH?

Almost every semester, I will have a student who will email me asking to be excused because of the death of a loved one, most often a grandparent. It makes me more sensitive as I teach about death, and more appreciative of the Book of Mormon. I often share with my students a sobering experience.

One afternoon, after visiting a friend in the hospital, I was walking down the long corridor to go home when I heard an announcement over the hospital's PA system: "We need a Mormon elder on the third floor. If you are a Mormon elder, please come to the nurse's station." I was nearby, so I went to the nurse's station and told them I was a Mormon elder. Another young man had also arrived, and a nurse motioned us to follow her. She stopped around the corner from the patient's room and said quietly but rather abruptly, "This woman is going to die today, and she wants a blessing from a Mormon elder." Then she walked us to the doorway and departed. Needless to say, that was a sobering moment for me and my new companion.

"Uh, would you like to take this one, Elder?" was my first thought, I confess.

I'll finish the story in a moment, but at this point in the account, I love to ask my students, "What happens to us when we die?" I suppose that everyone who has ever lost a loved one or who has contemplated death has also pondered that question. A Christian website described the wide range of opinions on the subject:

> Within the Christian faith, there is a significant amount of confusion regarding what happens after death. Some hold that after death, everyone "sleeps" until the final judgment, after which everyone will be sent to heaven or hell. Others believe that at the moment of death, people are instantly judged and sent to their eternal destinations. Still others claim that when people die, their souls/spirits are sent to a "temporary" heaven or hell, to await the final resurrection, the final judgment, and then the finality of their eternal destination. ("What happens after death?," GotQuestions.org, accessed August 22, 2019)

Does the Book of Mormon offer any clarification on the subject? It does, and it helped me in the hospital that day. After a quick spiritual inventory and plea for heavenly help, we took a deep breath and gave the woman a blessing. She was unconscious, but a loved one—her husband or her boyfriend, we presumed—was in the room with us. In addition to offering a blessing, we hoped to offer some comforting words, and I was so grateful for the Book of Mormon at that time! The Book of Mormon has some wonderful, specific, clarifying teachings about what happens after death. One of the references I was thankful I had memorized for just such an occasion appears in Alma 40:11–12:

> Now, concerning the state of the soul between death and the resurrection—Behold, it has been made known unto me by an angel, that the spirits of all men, as soon as they are departed from this mortal body, yea, the spirits of all men, whether they be good or evil, are taken home to that God who gave them life. And then shall it come to pass, that the spirits of those who are righteous are received into a state of happiness, which is called paradise, a state of rest, a state of peace, where they shall rest from all their troubles and from all care, and sorrow.

These comforting words describe the spirit world, or, in other words, "the state of the soul between death and the resurrection." So the spirit does not "sleep" until the final judgment, but the righteous spirits go to paradise. In the next verse, Alma explains that the wicked shall be cast into "outer darkness" (which we normally refer to as spirit prison). Alma continues, "Thus they remain in this state, as well as the righteous in paradise, until the time of their resurrection" (Alma 40:13–14).

So the order of events in this part of the plan of redemption is this: mortal death, spirit world (either paradise or prison), resurrection, final judgment. "But wait, Brother Bytheway," my students have asked, "in the verse we just read, it says the spirits are 'taken home to that God who gave them life.' So don't we see God when we die?" Yup, Alma does say that. He's using language similar to

Ecclesiastes 12:7, "The spirit shall return unto God who gave it." I add one word in my scriptures for clarity—*eventually*. Yes, we are taken home to God, eventually, and spiritual death will be overcome for all when we appear at the Final Judgment. For some, that reunion with God will be only temporary. Hopefully, we will be able to stay and remain in God's presence eternally.

Why is this an important point? Why does it matter whether we go immediately to God or not? Some of my students have asked, "What about all those near-death experiences where people die and say they were greeted by a being of light?" Excellent question. I believe they are probably greeted by an angel or perhaps a deceased relative—I don't know for sure. I have read a few books on so-called near-death experiences and have been fascinated by what I have read and how often the experiences of these people correspond with scriptural teachings (see Brent and Wendy Top, *Glimpses beyond Death's Door* [2012], for example).

So although Alma says we are taken home to God, we must consider the other dozen or so references in the Book of Mormon, which clarify that our return to the presence of God is a *post-resurrection* reunion. So being "taken home to God" at death must mean something other than being immediately restored to God's presence. We are taken back to those godly realms but not directly into God's presence at the time of death.

The scriptures are pretty clear. As we know from the Book of Mormon and other sources, there's still a lot of work to do in the spirit world before we are restored to God's presence (see Alma 11:41; 40:23; Helaman 14:7).

THE RESURRECTION

After our stay in the spirit world, we will be resurrected. Is the Book of Mormon the only book of scripture that talks about the Resurrection? No, but it is a bit more specific about what *resurrection* actually means. The Apostle Paul, after mentioning that there are bodies celestial and terrestrial, describes how our mortal bodies are buried, or "sown," and will be raised, or will come forth as resurrected bodies:

> So also is the resurrection of the dead. It is sown in corruption; it is raised in incorruption: it is sown in dishonour; it is raised in glory: it is sown in weakness; it is raised in power: it is sown a natural body; it is raised a spiritual body. There is a natural body, and there is a spiritual body. (1 Corinthians 15:42–44)

Here is the source of some of the debate in the Christian world about the Resurrection. What is a "spiritual body"? Is it a physical, tangible body? Can you touch it? Or is a "spiritual body" simply a spirit? The *Christian Book of Why* states:

> The body that ascends to heaven will be a "spiritual" body—one not bound by space and time as it was while living on earth. St. Paul wrote that at death we sow a "physical" body and reap a "spiritual" body (1 Corinthians 15:44). Exactly what this "spiritual" body will look like, no one knows for certain. (John C. McCallister, *The Christian Book of Why* [1983], 85)

But there is more to the confusion. The influence of Greek philosophy on Christian understanding was huge in the early Church. The philosophers looked upon anything physical as coarse, unrefined, and subject to decay; why would anyone even want a physical body? Let alone God? The idea that God would be physical in nature was foolishness to them.

So here's where we need some help. What is a spirit body, what is a spiritual body, and what is a resurrected body? While some may assume a spiritual body is something less than a physical, tangible body, the Book of Mormon offers more clarity. Alma continued:

> The soul shall be restored to the body, and the body to the soul; yea, and every limb and joint shall be restored to its body; yea, even a hair of the head shall not be lost; but all things shall be restored to their proper and perfect frame. (Alma 40:23)

So if "every limb and joint" will be restored, then resurrected bodies have limbs and joints! (For some reason, *soul* and *spirit* are used interchangeably in the Book of Mormon, so for clarity you can substitute *spirit* for *soul* in the verse above.) Amulek taught the Resurrection earlier using the word *spirit*:

> The spirit and the body shall be reunited again in its perfect form; both limb and joint shall be restored to its proper frame, even as we now are at this time; and we shall be brought to stand before God, knowing even as

we know now, and have a bright recollection of all our guilt. (Alma 11:43)

Now, what is a "spiritual body"? After describing in detail that a resurrected body is indeed physical and tangible, Amulek says:

> I say unto you that this mortal body is raised to an immortal body, that is from death, even from the first death unto life, that they can die no more; their spirits uniting with their bodies, never to be divided; thus the whole becoming spiritual and immortal, that they can no more see corruption. (Alma 11:45)

Aha, did you see it there? "The whole becoming *spiritual*." That's the same word Paul used in 1 Corinthians 15. So a spiritual body is still a physical body. Also, notice that Amulek said "never to be divided," which is an important point. If we say that resurrection is the reuniting of body and spirit, that's what happens to someone who is raised from the dead. Resurrection, then, is the reuniting of body and spirit "never to be divided," making impossible any sort of reincarnation doctrine (of returning to earth and dying once again).

The Doctrine and Covenants confirms the idea of a resurrected body being a "spiritual body": "For notwithstanding they die, they also shall rise again, a spiritual body" (D&C 88:27). President Joseph Fielding Smith spoke of those who deny the physical resurrection and addressed the difference between the spirit body and spiritual body:

When Paul spoke of the *spiritual* body, he had no reference at all to the *spirit* body, and there they have made their mistake. They have confused the spiritual body, or, in other words, the body quickened by the spirit, with the body of the spirit alone. They think that those who believe in the resurrection of the literal body believe that it shall be raised again, quickened by blood, which is not the case. . . .

After the resurrection from the dead our bodies will be spiritual bodies, but they will be bodies that are tangible, bodies that have been purified, but they will nevertheless be bodies of flesh and bones. They will not be *blood bodies*. They will no longer be quickened by blood but quickened by the spirit which is eternal, and they shall become immortal and shall never die. (*Doctrines of Salvation,* 3 vols. [1954–1956], 2:285; emphasis in original)

A mortal body is flesh and blood, while a resurrected body is flesh and bone, "quickened" by the spirit. Remember that Jesus taught, "Handle me, and see; for a spirit hath not flesh and bones, as ye see me have" (Luke 24:39). Notice the Savior used the words *flesh and bones*, not *flesh and blood*. A resurrected body of flesh and bone is a spiritual body.

POWER OF RESURRECTION

The Book of Mormon contains a phrase regarding the Resurrection that increases my testimony. Many of my students are enrolled in a required class called Physical Science, in which they are taught, among other things, about the Second Law of Thermodynamics, or entropy. Ever heard of that? It is the idea that everything goes from a state of order to disorder, or everything breaks down over time. Brother Tad R. Callister, in writing about the Resurrection, observed:

> Jacob pointed out that absent some offsetting power, "This flesh must have laid down to rot and to crumble to its mother earth" (2 Nephi 9:7). This is a manifestation of entropy, which is the process of going from a more organized state to a less organized state. Hugh Nibley observes, "Without the resurrection, entropy— the good old Second Law of Thermodynamics—must take over" (*Approaching Zion* [1989], 555). It is no surprise that Jacob, who observed that "death hath passed upon all men," also observed that "there must needs be a *power* of resurrection" (2 Nephi 9:6; emphasis added). There had to be some reversing power to thwart the inexorable march of decay, decomposition, and ultimate disorder. Decay and death are constant forces, or powers, wreaking havoc upon God's creations. (*The Infinite Atonement* [2000], 167)

Isn't it interesting that the Book of Mormon uses the phrase *power of resurrection*? A knowledge of the true nature of death and the "power of resurrection" can give us great hope that entropy can be overcome, and with power. While speaking of the people of Ammon, Mormon reported:

> They never did look upon death with any degree of terror, for their hope and views of Christ and the

resurrection; therefore, death was swallowed up to them
by the victory of Christ over it. (Alma 27:28)

Does the Book of Mormon answer every question
about what happens after we die? No. In fact, much of
our understanding of the specifics of the plan of redemption come from other Latter-day scripture. The Bible has
more references to the premortal existence than the Book
of Mormon, which only hints of a premortal existence in
Alma 13, and the Book of Mormon says essentially nothing about the three degrees of glory. Most of what we
know about the premortal existence comes from the Pearl
of Great Price (in the book of Abraham). Activity in both
parts of the spirit world is addressed in D&C 137 and 138,
and more specifics about the type of resurrected bodies we
will have are found in D&C 76.

The Book of Mormon gives us hope and precious information about the spirit world and the Resurrection,
a literal, physical resurrection by which we will have our
bodies again. Now, it might be a good idea to remember
that beautiful verse in Alma 40 in case you ever hear an
announcement like I heard as you are leaving the hospital.

Chapter Eight

EXPOSING THE ENEMIES OF CHRIST

An intriguing question is a gift. When a student asks a tough one, the whole class goes into "search mode," and we put our collective heads together searching for an answer. Here's a good one:

If the scriptures teach us to "say nothing but repentance unto this generation" (D&C 11:9), why would the scriptures give any airtime to anti-Christs? If Korihor's arguments were so persuasive that many good people were deceived, why would we preserve those arguments for a new generation? Shouldn't we have left them buried?

Anyone who has read the Book of Mormon knows that space on the plates was precious, that engraving upon them was difficult, and that we are getting a fraction of everything that happened in the New World. "I cannot include a hundredth part . . ." is a phrase repeated by the record keepers throughout the text.

Which makes this student's question even more interesting: Why in the world would we give Korihor a new platform in our day? With space on plates being so precious, why would we give Sherem any time to talk about his false philosophy? Or Nehor? Or the Zoramites? All good questions. President Ezra Taft Benson gave a wonderful answer:

> The Book of Mormon exposes the enemies of Christ. It confounds false doctrines and lays down contention. (See 2 Ne. 3:12.) It fortifies the humble followers of Christ against the evil designs, strategies, and doctrines of the devil in our day. The type of apostates in the Book of Mormon are similar to the type we have today. God, with his infinite foreknowledge, so molded the Book of Mormon that we might see the error and know how to combat false educational, political, religious, and philosophical concepts of our time. (*Teachings of Presidents of the Church: Ezra Taft Benson* [2014], 132)

That is the reason for allowing anti-Christs to preach their false doctrines on the plates—to expose them as enemies of Christ.

It is tempting to paint all of the Lord's adversaries with the same brush, but the Book of Mormon will not allow that. The enemies of Christ occupy a continuum from "there is no God" at one end to "there is a God but you're all doing it wrong" at the other, with a few gradations in between. That's the genius of it—there will be a broad spectrum of enemies of Christ in our day as well.

KORIHOR: "THERE IS NO GOD"

An entire chapter, and in fact one of the longer chapters in the Book of Mormon, is the story of Korihor: his philosophy, his confrontation with Church leaders, and his ultimate confession and demise. First of all, Korihor had a lot to say about believers in God and in Christ. He described them as bound, foolish, yoked, frenzied, and deranged, among other things. In addition, he taught that:

- "Ye cannot know of things which ye do not see" (in modern language, "seeing is believing")
- "Every man prospered according to his genius" (myth of the "self-made man")
- "Every man conquered according to his strength" ("survival of the fittest")
- "Whatsoever a man did was no crime" (there is no such thing as "right" and "wrong")
- "When a man was dead, that was the end thereof" (there is no ultimate judgment, and therefore no accountability for our choices) (Alma 30:15–18)

Those who believed Korihor began to make what we call "Kori-horrible" decisions. (Dad jokes are my specialty.)

It's interesting, and kind of sad, that Korihor's teachings caused many to "lift up their heads in their wickedness" and led them to "commit whoredoms" (Alma 30:18). When we are ashamed or repentant, we bow our heads. By contrast, the imagery of the people *lifting up* their heads in wickedness is a body language that says, "Really? You mean it's not wrong to do this? Alrighty then." Emboldened by Korihor's philosophy, they "lift up their heads" in sin.

Some of my students have wondered how, since there was "no law against a man's belief" (Alma 30:11), the people were justified in binding Korihor and carrying him before the high priest and the chief judges of the land. It comes down to the difference between beliefs and behavior. My personal opinion is that Korihor was *participating* in the whoredoms he was excusing, as well as causing others to commit whoredoms. Although there was freedom to believe whatever you wanted, it was still against the law to commit adultery in that day (see Alma 30:10), and perhaps to cause others to do so. Therefore, Korihor was breaking the law by participating in illegal behavior and was subject to its penalties.

One of Korihor's accusations that is still being used in the latter days is his claim that the leaders are glutting themselves with the labors of the people's hands, so that the people "durst not enjoy their rights and privileges" (Alma 30:27). One of Satan's tactics is to paint those who are willing to obey the commandments of God as gullible victims or mindless sheep who are not "enjoying their rights" or are being deprived of their rights by leaders with bad motives. Korihor falsely accuses the leaders as being nothing more than controlling zealots who won't let the people live their lives as they want. It's an old strategy that still works today.

Some are so confused when they see others deliberately choosing to obey a set of commandments, they assume there must be some kind of mind control or cultural coercion going on. They cannot understand why anyone would willingly keep all those rules. Why would we? It reminds me of a saying I heard: "Those who danced were thought to be quite insane by those who could not hear the music."

ately, Korihor demanded a sign. Jesus taught that and [notice this] *adulterous* generation seeketh after a sign" (Matthew 16:4; emphasis added). How interesting! Fits perfectly here, doesn't it? Why is sign seeking equated with adultery? Think about it—a sign seeker wants proof or evidence of something without any effort or searching. An adulterer wants the privileges of marriage without any commitment. Both involve a similar "something-for-nothing" mentality.

Alma's brilliant response to Korihor's demand for a sign was to turn the tables on Korihor: "What evidence have ye that there is no God, or that Christ cometh not?" (Alma 30:40). That's a great question. Alma then lists what I call a hierarchy of testimony (Alma 30:39, 44):

- "I know there is a God, and also that Christ shall come"
- "Ye have the testimony of all these thy brethren"
- "And also all the holy prophets"
- "The scriptures are laid before thee"
- "All things denote there is a God"

Notice he starts with personal testimony, continues with the testimonies of others, and ends with evidences in nature and creation. Sometimes we get those reversed, but perhaps we are being taught that in our interactions with others we should always start with personal testimony.

Ultimately, Korihor is struck dumb (and deaf, evidently, since others have to write messages to him to communicate), and Korihor finally admits "he always knew there was a God" (Alma 30:52). What he had taught was so pleasing to the carnal mind that he had much "success," as he put it, and it led to his death. This long chapter ends with an important "thus we see . . ."

> And thus we see the end of him who perverteth the ways of the Lord; and thus we see that the devil will not support his children at the last day, but doth speedily drag them down to hell. (Alma 30:60)

The devil would like to convince us that he is an ally. Some have fallen for it, and they deliberately use Satanic symbols to market their materials (on posters, ads, and merchandise). Others have repeated Korihor's arguments in modern, sophisticated language. But the devil will not support his children at the last day, since he wants us to be as miserable as he is. Lehi warned about the power of the devil, who "seeketh that all men might be miserable like unto himself" (2 Nephi 2:27). That lesson, or what we might call "Satan's mission statement," was worth the space on the plates, in Mormon's inspired judgment.

NEHOR: "NO NEED TO FEAR OR TREMBLE"

This Nehor character is one of the scariest in the Book of Mormon, and although he comes and goes in only fifteen verses of one chapter (Alma 1), his influence continues for many chapters.

While Korihor said there is no God, Nehor taught something different. He taught that there *is* a God, however:

- Priests should become "popular" (or supported by money from the populace)
- All mankind should be saved at the last day
- They need not fear or tremble
- The Lord created all men
- The Lord has redeemed all men
- In the end, all men should have eternal life (Alma 1:3–4)

Why would this philosophy be so popular? Sounds pretty good, pretty easy, doesn't it? Nehor gained followers because his theology didn't require anything at all! Elder L. Tom Perry observed:

> Nehor's words appealed to many of the people; they were easy words because they required neither obedience nor sacrifice. As we face many decisions in life, the easy and popular messages of the world will seem appealing. But . . . it will take great courage to choose the right. (*Living with Enthusiasm* [1996], 108–9)

No obedience, no sacrifice (and no meetings, I'll bet), but, as my friend Brad Wilcox wisely observed, "A God who asks nothing of us is making nothing of us" (*The Continuous Conversion* [2013], 17). Imagine a child saying, "If my parents really loved me, they'd let me skip school and play video games all day." Does that sound loving? Does it sound caring? Sounds more like indifference. Interesting how a doctrine of the devil can be clothed in a language of "love." But love cannot destroy law or accountability.

Ideas similar to Nehor's abound today. Some, while

believing in God, may preach that "he loves us so much that I think he's just going to save everyone." Or another one I've heard, "I don't think God is all about punishment, I think he's all about love." Isn't that sweet? Yeah, it sounds loving, but it also throws any sort of accountability for our behavior out the window.

Nehor didn't even mention commandments—or any standard of conduct of any kind at all—in his popular theology.

Nehor's preaching became so popular, in fact, that people began to support him and give him money. So he bought himself a new set of costly apparel and started his own church. "Priestcrafts," Nephi taught, "are that men preach and set themselves up for a light unto the world, that they may get gain and praise of the world; but they seek not the welfare of Zion" (2 Nephi 26:29).

One of my religion teachers, Joseph Fielding McConkie, observed that when the moon blocks out the light of the sun, we call that an eclipse. When anyone or anything blocks out the Son of God, we might call that a spiritual eclipse. "Don't ever be a spiritual eclipse!" Brother McConkie taught us that day, and it changed my life. Nehor, rather than pointing others to Christ, was pointing to himself, thus blocking out Christ.

Eventually, Nehor was confronted by Gideon, a teacher in the Church of God, and Nehor, unable to with-stand Gideon's words, drew his sword and began to smite Gideon. And why not? If there are no commandments and no accountability, you can just smite anyone who disagrees with you. God will save us all anyway, so who cares about murder, right? In the end we'll all have eternal life. If someone disagrees with you, just kill them. That's a frightening philosophy.

Nehor's "God will save everyone regardless . . ." doctrine was preserved on plates to expose another false enemy of Christ in the latter days. But it can also spark an important discussion—how does God balance his love with his law? To help address that question, I ask my students to read an address by Elder Dallin H. Oaks called "Love and Law" from the October 2009 general conference. It's on your Gospel Library app—you know what to do.

SHEREM: "OVERTHROW THE DOCTRINE OF CHRIST"

Prophecy is a difficult concept for some, including some of the enemies of Christ. Sherem, like Korihor, said that you cannot know of things to come. Unlike Korihor, Sherem believed that there was a God, but that the law of Moses was the right way to worship. But what is the law of Moses? Can it really be separated from Christ? Here is my favorite definition:

> The law of Moses was as one grand prophecy of Christ inasmuch as it testified of the salvation to be obtained in and through his atoning blood. Jesus was the fulfillment of that prophecy. (Joseph Fielding McConkie and Robert L. Millet, *Doctrinal Commentary on the Book of Mormon*, 4 vols. [1987–1992], 3:250)

Yes, the law of Moses is a "grand prophecy of Christ," and, for the most part, the people of God in the Book of

Mormon understood that connection. Sherem is the lone exception. He accused Jacob, saying:

> And ye have led away much of this people that they pervert the right way of God, and keep not the law of Moses which is the right way; and convert the law of Moses into the worship of a being which ye say shall come many hundred years hence. And now behold, I, Sherem, declare unto you that this is blasphemy; for no man knoweth of such things; for he cannot tell of things to come. (Jacob 7:7)

Sherem sought for a sign and, like Korihor, received one. He was eventually executed for slaying Gideon. What should we do with this story? It is interesting to imagine what it would be like to live before Christ had come, and to be required to exercise faith in someone who hadn't lived on earth yet—and faith in an Atonement for sin that hadn't been made yet. Perhaps this is why some struggle with the idea of prophecy.

For us, we look backward in time, and we have evidence that Jesus existed. What year is it? Two thousand what? And when did we start counting the years over again? Oh, yeah, at the birth of Christ. Art, literature, and music have all been heavily influenced by Jesus of Nazareth. Was he really the Son of God? That's what we believe, and while others do not, it is impossible for them to deny that someone named Jesus really lived and changed the course of history.

In our dispensation, our testimony is that living prophets exist today. Some would rather stick with past prophets and not allow for any new ones. Old prophets stay safely in the past, where we can interpret them as we please without any fear of them challenging our interpretation.

Our testimony is that Jesus Christ really does live and speak to prophets today, and that because we have prophets, there are those who really can know of things to come.

OTHER FALSE PHILOSOPHIES
MENTIONED IN THE BOOK OF MORMON

Besides the teachings of Korihor, Nehor, and Sherem, other false philosophies are mentioned in the Book of Mormon, many in one of Nephi's final chapters, 2 Nephi 28.

If there is no God, then why not "eat, drink, and be merry, for tomorrow we die" (2 Nephi 28:7)? That was Korihor's philosophy. But what if there is a God? Another philosophy says "Okay, there is a God, but his punishments aren't too bad, so we can still pop the corks and get this party started":

> And there shall also be many which shall say: Eat, drink, and be merry; nevertheless, fear God—he will justify in committing a little sin; yea, lie a little, take the advantage of one because of his words, dig a pit for thy neighbor; there is no harm in this; and do all these things, for tomorrow we die; and if it so be that we are guilty, God will beat us with a few stripes, and at last we shall be saved in the kingdom of God. (2 Nephi 28:8)

Chapter 28 of 2 Nephi is a remarkable prophetic chapter. It speaks of the day when the Book of Mormon will come forth and of the various attitudes toward God that will exist in that day. These include a wide range of false philosophies and churches and organizations that will:

Create contention (v. 4)

Rely on learning, not on the Holy Ghost (v. 4)

Deny the existence and power of God (v. 5)

Deny miracles (v. 6)

Teach that death is the end (v. 7)

Teach that God will allow some sin (v. 8)

Teach that God will save everyone (v. 8)

Promote a "sin now, repent later" mind-set (v. 8)

Encourage pride (vv. 9, 12)

Rob the poor because of excessive spending (v. 13)

Promote whoredoms and immorality (v. 14)

Emphasize riches (v. 15)

Twist the truth (v. 15)

Revile that which is good (v. 16)

Promote anger (v. 19)

Pacify and lull people into believing all is well (v. 21)

Cheat souls (v. 21)

Lead souls carefully down to hell (v. 21)

Use flattery (v. 22)

Teach there is no devil or hell (v. 22)

Say there is no need for new scripture (v. 29)

Teach to trust in man, not in God (v. 31)

Speaking of the enemies of Christ we will face in the latter days, President Boyd K. Packer gave a solemn prophetic warning that includes dangers not only from outside the Church but from within:

Atheists and agnostics make nonbelief their religion and today organize in unprecedented ways to attack faith and belief. They are now organized, and they pursue political power. You will be hearing much about them and from them. Much of their attack is indirect in mocking the faithful, in mocking religion.

The types of Sherem, Nehor, and Korihor live among us today (see Jacob 7:1–21; Alma 1:1–15; 30:6–60). Their arguments are not so different from those in the Book of Mormon.

You who are young will see many things that will try your courage and test your faith. All of the mocking does not come from outside of the Church. Let me say that again: all of the mocking does not come from out-side of the Church. Be careful that you do not fall into the category of mocking. ("Finding Ourselves in Lehi's Dream," *Ensign*, August 2010)

I remember hearing about a seminary teacher who asked the class to list some of Satan's lies on the black-board. Some of them come straight out of 2 Nephi 28:

- There is no devil
- There is no hell
- There is no such thing as right and wrong
- There is no need to repent and change

But the one that stuck out to me was this one:

- There is no *hurry*

If there is one impression we've probably all been left with over the past few years, it is that the Lord is "has-tening his work" (see D&C 88:73). In modern language, we've got to get our act together, not someday, but today. As one old saying puts it, "The best time to plant a tree is twenty years ago; the second best time is now." There *is* a hurry. There is a sense of urgency. Amulek pleaded:

And now, as I said unto you before, as ye have had so many witnesses, therefore, I beseech of you that ye do not procrastinate the day of your repentance until the end; for after this day of life, which is given us to prepare for eternity, behold, if we do not improve our time while in this life, then cometh the night of darkness wherein there can be no labor performed. (Alma 34:33)

"Know your enemy" is great advice for military planners who spend a great deal of time and treasure gathering intelligence to figure out the enemy's plans and tactics. The Book of Mormon teaches us how to prepare for attacks from the enemy of our souls as well. In my own efforts of gathering intelligence on the enemies of Christ, I prepared this chart:

	SHEREM (Jacob 7)	NEHOR (Alma 1)	ZORAMITES (Alma 31)	KORIHOR (Alma 30)
Personal Traits	Knowledge of language, power of speech, flatterer	A large, strong man, wore costly apparel	Wealthy, well-dressed, had cast out the poor	Used great, swelling, flattering words
Existence of God	Yes	Yes	Yes	No
Regarding Prophecy	One cannot know of things to come	Not mentioned	Not mentioned	One cannot know of things to come
Means of Salvation	Law of Moses	All will be redeemed	Zoramites are "elected" to be saved	Death is the end; no such thing as right and wrong
Regarding Christ	No Christ; law of Moses saves	All will be saved; no mention of Christ	There will be no Christ	No Christ

To me, one of the more interesting rows on this chart involves the personality traits of the enemies of Christ. If these traits were important enough for the Book of Mormon writers to mention, they must be important for us to notice. Today, the influence of Hollywood celebrities and icons of popular culture includes individuals with great personal talents of magnetism, attractiveness, and persuasion.

When Jacob first encountered Sherem, he noted that Sherem "had hope to shake me from the faith," but because of Jacob's relationship with the Lord, because of his ability to get his own answers to prayers, because of his own testimony, Jacob assured, "I had heard the voice of the Lord speaking unto me in very word, from time to time; wherefore, I could not be shaken" (Jacob 7:5).

So how do we prepare for our encounters with these enemies of Christ? How can we say with confidence, "I cannot be shaken?" Jacob gives us the answer. We must learn, like Jacob, to receive our own answers, to receive our own witnesses, to "hear the voice of the Lord" through our own reading, studying, and pondering so that we too will not be shaken by the enemies of Christ.

Chapter Nine

CONVERTED TO WHAT?

"If it's not too personal, may I ask, how many of you are converts?" It's wonderful to be able to draw upon a classroom of individuals with different backgrounds, cultures, languages, and histories who found their way to The Church of Jesus Christ of Latter-day Saints. Those of us who were baptized at eight years old look with admiration on those who discovered the gospel on their own, or who were brought to it through the efforts of others. As the discussion concludes, we come to the realization that all of us must be converted, and we are therefore all converts. But what does *convert* mean?

If you looked around your house, you could probably find a dozen items called "converters," and so could I. I pack an electrical converter with me when I travel to change three-prong plugs to two. I have software on my laptop that converts WAV files to mp3 files so I can listen to them on my phone. My car has a catalytic converter in the exhaust system. We routinely convert metric measurements to American ones, and vice versa. What does it mean to convert something? Simple answer: to change

97

it into something else. The dictionary.com definitions of *convert* are:

- to change (something) into a different form or properties; transmute; transform.
- to cause to adopt a different religion, political doctrine, opinion, etc., as in "convert the heathen."

We all know converting is about changing, but changing into what? *That* is the critical question. I know how to convert electrical plugs and audio clips, but when it comes to human beings, to sons and daughters of God, shouldn't it be crystal clear what are we converting to? Shouldn't the object of our conversion be clearly known? Shouldn't there be absolutely no confusion on the subject?

We have probably heard the phrase a thousand times: "She was converted to the Church," or "I am a convert to the Church," and so forth. I have heard those phrases and probably used them myself, but is that the object of our conversion? The Church? Is that what the Lord wants us converted to?

The Book of Mormon taught me something wonderful when it comes to conversion. It contains many stories of conversion, but it never uses the phrase "convert to the Church." Never. The phrase it does use—and the fact that it is consistent throughout—should send us a very strong message. You'll see it immediately in the following list, and it may forever change the phrase you use when speaking of "converts." Ready? (In order of appearance):

Alma 19:16—Abish, she having been *converted unto the Lord*

Alma 22:23—his whole household were *converted unto the Lord*

Alma 23:3—the king had been *converted unto the Lord,* and all his household

Alma 24:6—the people who had been *converted unto the Lord*

Alma 53:10—they had been *converted unto the Lord*

3 Nephi 1:22—the more part of the people did believe, and were *converted unto the Lord*

3 Nephi 2:12—the Lamanites who had become *converted unto the Lord*

3 Nephi 7:21—there were but few who were *converted unto the Lord*

4 Nephi 1:2—the people were all *converted unto the Lord*

Okay, that's nine references, but I held the tenth one until last because it helps answer the question of the role of the Church in our *conversion unto the Lord:*

3 Nephi 28:23—and they were *converted unto the Lord,* and were united unto the church of Christ

The object of our conversion, the type of being we are trying to become and be converted to, is the Lord. He is the object of our conversion, the one we look to and try to emulate. One of my favorite "keep me focused on the right thing" scriptures was spoken by the Lord and is found in D&C 19:23:

Learn of me, and listen to my words; walk in the meekness of my Spirit, and you shall have peace in me.

Notice the "me, my, my, and me" in that verse. Now, substitute "the Church" in those places where it says "me" and "my," and you'll notice that it loses power. Don't get me wrong, I love the Church. I love it! The Church is the place where we unite to worship with others who are also trying to become like the Lord. But we are to be converted to Christ, not to the Church.

What is the role of Christ's Church, then? Elder D. Todd Christofferson taught:

In this discussion of the Church as the body of Christ, we must always bear in mind two things. One, we do not strive for conversion to the Church but to Christ and His gospel, a conversion that is facilitated by the Church. The Book of Mormon expresses it best when it says that the people "were converted unto the Lord, and were united unto the church of Christ" [3 Nephi 28:23]. ("Why the Church," *Ensign*, November 2015)

Dr. Stephen R. Covey wrote a book in the late 1980s titled *The Seven Habits of Highly Effective People*. It quickly became a worldwide bestseller and one of the greatest personal development books of all time. Brother Covey was a former mission president and a faithful member of the Church, and he also wrote a book for members of the Church called *6 Events: The Restoration Model for Solving Life's Problems*. That book greatly increased my understanding of the role of the Lord and the role of the Church in our conversion to Christ.

Brother Covey's thesis was that the events of the Restoration of the gospel were not only wonderful and world-changing, but the very order in which they occurred has a message for our most important priorities and is like a formula for solving life's problems. Each of the monumental events answers a question. In a nutshell:

1. The First Vision: "Who is God, and who am I?"
2. The restoration of the gospel through the Book of Mormon: "Whose am I?"
3. The restoration of the priesthood: "How can I receive Christ?"
4. The restoration of the Church: "Where do I go to receive Christ?"
5. The restoration of the keys of salvation for the living and the dead: "What is the work I should do in life?"
6. The restoration of the temple ordinances: "Why did God bring about the Restoration?" (Stephen R. Covey, *6 Events: The Restoration Model for Solving Life's Problems* [2004], 224)

You may want to read that list again slowly. I think it's a brilliant observation. The answers to the first two questions are about our relationship with God and Christ, the real object of our conversion. The Church is down the list a ways at number four.

This sequence has helped me in my ministering activities. I've realized that with some who are no longer meeting with us, my focus and my approach should be to go back to lesson one, to share the fundamental truth that God lives and loves us and is aware of our problems and challenges and pains, rather than to go directly to lesson four and ask, "Hey, how come you're not coming to church?"

I have a friend whose teenage daughter was struggling with the desire to attend church. One Sunday morning the daughter announced, "Dad, I'm not going to church today," and my friend in an inspired moment gulped and said, "Okay." Then he went to church without her and prayed his heart out that he was doing the right thing, as you might imagine. At one point, he came across a story in the Book of Mormon involving another father praying for his child and for his child's repentance and conversion. In the scriptural story, an angel appeared and told the son, "[Thy father] has prayed with much faith concerning thee that thou mightest . . ."

Sorry to interrupt, but what do you think the father prayed for? "That thou mightest come back to church"? No. Interestingly, that wasn't the prayer. I'll continue the words of the angel: ". . . that thou mightest be brought *to the knowledge of the truth*" (Mosiah 27:14; emphasis added). Alma the Elder was praying that his son would get lessons one and two, not lesson four.

That was an epiphany for my friend. The most important thing for his daughter was that she come to a knowledge of the truth. He, like Alma, had to turn things over to the Lord, to some degree, and trust that He would help her come to a knowledge of the truth. If that could happen, her being "united with the Church" would naturally follow, once she discovered the truth of lessons one and two, "Who am I?" and "Whose am I?"

I'm grateful to report that after a while my friend's daughter began attending church again. Some parents out there are still waiting for that return; our hearts ache for them, and we pray with them. I'm grateful to my friend and to the Book of Mormon for giving me the words to use while praying for my children and for others: *I pray that they may come to a knowledge of the truth!*

THE GREAT PRIVILEGE OF OUR CHURCH

What about the Church, then? Does the Book of Mormon address that? Yes it does, numerous times. Some read the Bible and debate about whether Jesus really organized a church. Some believe that to be spiritual doesn't require any sort of organization, and we all know that organized religion is becoming less popular these days.

You may have noticed, as I have, many comments about religion on bumper stickers.

MY RELIGION IS KINDNESS.

Yeah, kindness is awesome; I believe in that too. But is that the whole thing? Sounds wonderful, but is that all there is? (Oops, is it unkind of me to ask?)

I'M SPIRITUAL BUT NOT RELIGIOUS.

Many subscribe to this idea, seeing religion as a bunch of rules and too many meetings and obligations. They say the churches are full of hypocrites anyway. ("That's all right," someone responded, "we've got room for one more!")

TREES ARE THE ANSWER.

Don't laugh, I saw this bumper sticker. And it's totally true if you want to know where wood comes from.

LOVE IS THE ANSWER.

This is a good one too, and a top-forty song in the '80s, but what is the goal? The final outcome? Where do I learn about my identity and my eternal destiny? How do I know what God wants and expects from me? Or do I just love, love, love and stop asking the deeper questions?

Now, to be fair, one cannot fit a system of theology on a bumper sticker, so forgive me for having a little fun repeating the conversations I have with myself while in traffic. I'm all for kindness, spirituality, love, and even trees. But it is also unfair to dismiss organized religion with the brevity of a bumper sticker: "I don't believe in organized religion, so I'll just be kind."

If we are sincerely interested in finding out more about God and if He knows us and cares about us, we begin to ask questions like, "Who am I?" (Event One), "Whose am I?" (Event Two), "How do I receive Christ?" (Event Three), and "Where would I go to do that?" (Event Four).

Perhaps there really is a God, and perhaps he wants much, much more from me so that I can become much, much more. Perhaps he is more interested in my growth than he is in my comfort.

If the Lord really wants us to be united with the Church, then the question, "What is the Church for?" is a valid one. In writing this chapter, I listened intently to

Elder D. Todd Christofferson's October 2015 general conference talk, "Why the Church," and made my own list of the reasons he mentioned:

- Preach the good news of the gospel of Jesus Christ and administer the ordinances of salvation (even to the spirits of the dead)
- Create a community of Saints who will sustain, teach, and edify one another
- Experience application of divine doctrine
- Be strengthened by association of members
- Be in a position to be reproved of sin and error
- Achieve needful things that cannot be accomplished by individuals or smaller groups
- Make ordinances available to all of God's children
- Preserve the purity of the Savior's doctrine and the integrity of his saving ordinances
- Judge worthiness of those who seek ordinances
- Identify falsehood
- Safeguard and publish God's revelations
- Prepare for the return and millennial rule of Jesus Christ

I think one of my favorites in that comprehensive list is "Experience application of divine doctrine." In other words, try as hard as we might, we are likely going to offend and receive offense, we're going to have to learn to forgive and ask forgiveness, we're going to trespass and have others trespass against us, and the divine doctrine of the Lord will teach us how to act and react in a community of Saints called the Church. It's easy to talk about kindness and to stick the word on your bumper, but when you interact with real people who have real problems, you get a real opportunity to practice the kindness you preach. And that real opportunity comes as part of the Church.

At one time I served as a bishop, and I never really knew when I extended a call or a release if I was doing it right. If I didn't release someone with the proper amount of gratitude, or have them sustained with the proper amount of gusto, I hoped they would forgive me. I hoped they would follow this advice from President Boyd K. Packer:

> All of us carry excess baggage around from time to time, but the wisest ones among us don't carry it for very long. They get rid of it.
>
> Some of it you have to get rid of without really solving the problem. Some things that ought to be put in order are not put in order because you can't control them.
>
> Often, however, the things we carry are petty, even stupid. If you are still upset after all these years because Aunt Clara didn't come to your wedding reception, why don't you grow up? Forget it.
>
> If you brood constantly over some past mistake, settle it—look ahead.
>
> If the bishop didn't call you right—or release you right—forget it.
>
> If you resent someone for something he has done, or failed to do—forget it.
>
> We call that forgiveness. It is powerful spiritual medicine. The instructions for its use are found in the scriptures. (*That All May be Edified* [1982], 68)

Yes, in a community of Saints, situations will arise in which we must "apply divine doctrine" and remember the object of our conversion. If the object of our conversion is the Church, then we might be shaken when we find imperfections in the Church, its members, or its policies, because the object of our conversion is on imperfect ground. If our conversion is to the Lord, we will be on solid ground when imperfections of members of the Church are manifest. We'll even expect those imperfections. Elder Jeffrey R. Holland advised:

> So be kind regarding human frailty—your own as well as that of those who serve with you in a Church led by volunteer, mortal men and women. Except in the case of His only perfect Begotten Son, imperfect people are all God has ever had to work with. That must be terribly frustrating to Him, but He deals with it. So should we. And when you see imperfection, remember that the limitation is *not* in the divinity of the work. ("Lord, I Believe," *Ensign*, May 2013)

Recently, the stake presidency in my area was reorganized, and the member of the Quorum of the Seventy who presided gave the congregation some counsel regarding our new leadership. "Please," he pleaded, "don't put them under a microscope. They can't take that, and neither can you. And if you see their children do something that raises your eyebrows, put them back down." Wonderful counsel. These men didn't ask for those callings, they were asked by the Lord, even in their imperfections.

Pahoran, the chief judge whose careful response to a

fiery Captain Moroni has landed him in the self-restraint hall of fame, used a phrase regarding the Church that I love:

> Therefore, my beloved brother, Moroni, let us resist evil, and whatsoever evil we cannot resist with our words, yea, such as rebellions and dissensions, let us resist them with our swords, that we may retain our freedom, that we may rejoice in the great privilege of our church, and in the cause of our Redeemer and our God. (Alma 61:14)

I love it! What a privilege to belong to the Church. And notice that the Lord and the Church are mentioned separately—the great *privilege of our church,* and the *cause of our Redeemer.*

Finally, in the closing chapters of the Book of Mormon, we find principles involved in ministering, roll keeping, holding meetings, and even convening Church courts (see Moroni 6). Clearly the Book of Mormon teaches that the Lord expects us to have a church organization, and I'm glad he does.

I cannot begin to imagine how much emptier my life would be without my brothers and sisters in the Church. These dear friends have seen me through tough times, and hopefully I have helped them through some of theirs. We have worshiped together, laughed together, cried together, mourned together, served together, raked leaves together, put away chairs together, and wondered what to do with excess funeral potatoes together. Over the decades, I have grown to realize how important my ward family is to me.

How empty would my life be if I had stayed home in my recliner all those years being "spiritual but not religious"?

I love the continuing revelation and the continuing changes in the Church. When I received my mission call many years ago, the Church over which President Spencer W. Kimball was presiding had three million members. At the time of this writing, the Church is more than five times larger, and more of its members are outside of North America than inside. It's a different Church, with a dramatically different demographic, so of course there will be constant changes and adjustments as the world and its challenges change.

However, one thing will never change: the object of our conversion. What manner of men and women ought we to be? Even as He is (see 3 Nephi 27:27). The Book of Mormon teaches me that Jesus organized a church, that he revealed things to the church leaders after his Resurrection, but that the object of our conversion is Christ. The Book of Mormon teaches me that day by day, I should strive to be converted unto the Lord, and week by week, united with the Church.

Chapter Ten

SCATTER AND GATHER

On this topic, I like to begin class with some interesting questions. Are you scattered or gathered? Have you ever been scattered? Are you more recently gathered? Is it possible to scatter again once you've been gathered? Can we ever say, as the hymn does, "*All* is safely gathered in"? ("Come Ye Thankful People," *Hymns* [1985], no. 94). Is it possible to be in church but going in the wrong direction? Is it possible to be in prison but going in the right direction? Yes! It's not about distance, it's about direction. All of us are part of the process of gathering.

As a parent, I am constantly gathering scattered things. If you were to ask me a few years ago, "What do you do as a dad?" I would have answered, "I look for shoes." I would have loved to give a more profound "proclamation on the family" answer in hushed tones while looking into the mid-distance, but mostly, I looked for shoes. And other scattered things. Gather the scattered Cap'n Crunch, gather the scattered crayons, gather the scattered Legos, and put them where they belong. *A place for everything and everything in its place.* That's the ideal. A place for everything and everything *out of place* is the real. At least at my house. Thankfully, my kids are getting older, and we now assist each other in the gathering.

Scatter, gather, scatter, gather, scatter, gather. It's kind of a tongue twister, and an accurate description of life on earth. It makes for some fun opening paragraphs, unless we're talking about scattered people—then it becomes fairly serious. People who are lost, people who don't know who they are, people who don't know that they are cared for, and people who don't know that precious blood has been shed for them—those people are an important scriptural topic, a "top-five" scriptural topic, in fact.

Anyone who reads the Book of Mormon will notice the theme of scattering and gathering, and anyone who listens in general conference will hear it too. Soon after President Russell M. Nelson was set apart as President of the Church, he and Sister Nelson spoke in their first Worldwide Youth Devotional. Of all the things they could have addressed, of the dozens of important things that might come to mind, please notice what they talked about:

> My dear young brothers and sisters, these surely *are* the latter days, and the Lord is hastening His work to gather Israel. That gathering is the most important thing taking place on earth today. Nothing else compares in magnitude, nothing else compares in importance, nothing else compares in majesty. . . .
>
> When we speak of the *gathering*, we are simply saying this fundamental truth: every one of our Heavenly Father's children, on both sides of the veil, deserves to

hear the message of the restored gospel of Jesus Christ. They decide for themselves if they want to know more.

What does the Book of Mormon offer in relation to the gathering? How can it help us? Oh, I'm so glad you asked. President Nelson continued:

> What will help you? As you continue to read daily from the Book of Mormon, you will learn the doctrine of the gathering, truths about Jesus Christ, His Atonement, and the fulness of His gospel not found in the Bible. The Book of Mormon is central to the gathering of Israel. In fact, if there were no Book of Mormon, the promised gathering of Israel would not occur. ("Hope of Israel," Worldwide Youth Devotional, June 3, 2018; emphasis in original)

This topic is dear to my heart for many reasons, but mostly because as I sit here at my word processor, my home feels a little emptier than usual. Two of my children are no longer at home scattering their shoes. They have been called to gather Israel full time. And how beautiful upon the mountains are their feet (hopefully with their formerly scattered shoes and socks on)! At the time of this writing, my oldest daughter is in France and my oldest son is in Iceland. Both of them are in what I might call "hunter" missions. I served in the Philippines, which I would call a "fisher" mission. I'll explain. In speaking of the gathering of Israel, the Lord told Jeremiah:

> Behold, I will send for many fishers, saith the Lord, and they shall fish them; and after will I send for many

hunters, and they shall hunt them from every mountain, and from every hill, and out of the holes of the rocks. (Jeremiah 16:16)

When I served in the Philippines, there were four missions and one announced temple site. Today, there are twenty-two missions and two temples, with five more announced. (It appears that things really picked up after I left.) In those beautiful islands, people were fairly open to listening to the missionaries. We could cast a net over the side, so to speak, and teach all week long, and we did.

My children are serving where the work is a little slower, more like hunting for someone who might be willing to listen, one soul at a time. What does this have to do with the Book of Mormon specifically?

As I've corresponded with my children on the other side of the Atlantic, I've discovered that my fisher mission experiences don't correspond very well to their hunter missions. However, as I've studied the Book of Mormon, I've been impressed that we each have a place to go to teach us how to assist in the gathering! This is just another reason why I've been so impressed with the genius of the Book of Mormon. Whether we are serving in a home ward, as a ministering brother or sister, or in any one of the hunter or fisher missions around the world, the Book of Mormon is arranged to help us with our questions.

• How do I talk to members who are slacking? *It's in there.*

- How do I talk to members who are doing great? *It's in there.*
- How do I talk to those who know nothing about Christ? *It's in there!*

There is not a one-size-fits-all approach to gathering Israel, except to let the Holy Spirit guide. Everyone is different, everyone is valued, and everyone is precious in the sight of God. The Book of Mormon offers examples and formulas for a wide range of gathering and ministering activities.

Let's look at those questions one at a time. First, what message is there for those members of the Church who are slacking?

ALMA 5: THE GET-YOUR-ACT-TOGETHER MESSAGE

Let's refresh our memories of the Book of Mormon story line: The four sons of Mosiah are going about trying to destroy the Church with the son of Alma the Elder. What a situation! The sons of the most high-profile leaders of the Church and the nation are together, rebelling against their fathers. An angel stops them in their tracks, scaring them nearly to death, and they repent. The four sons of Mosiah go on missions to the Lamanites, leaving King Mosiah with no son to confer the kingdom upon. He decides it might be a good time to start a new form of government, which we know as the "reign of the judges." Alma the Younger is appointed the first chief judge, but after a few years, he steps down to preach to his own people. Not "nonmembers," mind you, but Nephites who need the "get-your-act-together" message.

SCATTER AND GATHER 115

Alma 5 is Alma's message to the members in Zarahemla. It's a long chapter, sixty-two verses long, and reading Alma 5 is like reading a powerful general conference talk, a real call-to-action type message. It is clear that Alma is talking to members of the Church because he addresses them in the text as "my brethren of the church" (see verses 6, 14, and 54, for example).

Alma 5 has been called a "spiritual midterm" since it is composed of about fifty questions, such as: Are you stripped of pride? Are you stripped of envy? Do you make a mock of your brother? Have you received His image in your countenance? And so forth. One of my favorite questions is this one:

> And now behold, I say unto you, my brethren, if ye
> have experienced a change of heart, and if ye have felt
> to sing the song of redeeming love, I would ask, can ye
> feel so now? (Alma 5:26)

In other words, there was a time when you were so excited about the gospel of Jesus Christ that it made you want to *sing*! Do you still feel that way now? Are you making progress spiritually? If not, what has happened since then? Make a graph of your spiritual growth—which way are you trending? What have you been up to that has brought you to where you are now? Did you scatter yourself? What can you do to rekindle that fire? Answering those questions for ourselves requires some serious introspection. We can't gather Israel if we are not gathered ourselves!

If you or someone you love has "paused on some

plateaus long enough" (to use President Kimball's phrase from "Let Us Move Forward and Upward," *Ensign*, May 1979) and needs to move onward and upward, Alma 5 teaches an approach. Does anything I've written here make you want to read Alma's sixty-two-verse message? Good. Put this book down and go read Alma 5!

ALMA 7: THE MAY-THE-PEACE-OF-GOD-REST-UPON-YOU MESSAGE

Next, what message is in the Book of Mormon for those members of the Church who are doing pretty well?

When Alma leaves Zarahemla, he goes to a place called Gideon. Now, Alma could have been thinking to himself, "I gave a great talk in Zarahemla. I think it went over really well! I'm going to try it here too." But what if the people in Gideon were in a different place spiritually from those in Zarahemla? They were. The very fact that Alma teaches something so different in Gideon teaches us a wonderful lesson. As someone once said, "Rather than preparing a speech, prepare yourself to speak." We're not teaching a lesson, we're teaching *people*! And people are in different places spiritually and sometimes in need of different messages.

Alma begins his message in Gideon by stating, "I trust that ye are not in a state of so much unbelief as were your brethren; I trust that ye are not lifted up in the pride of your hearts" (Alma 7:6).

In Zarahemla, he talked about a lot of things, but in Gideon he says, "There is one thing which is more important than they all—for behold, the time is not far distant that the Redeemer liveth and cometh among his people" (Alma 7:7). I'll bet you could have heard a Zarahemla pin drop.

Can you feel the contrast? Those in Zarahemla got grilled, and those in Gideon heard prophecies about Christ! (What might that teach us about the kind of messages our prophets are sharing with us?) Alma continues:

> And behold, he shall be born of Mary, at Jerusalem which is the land of our forefathers, she being a virgin, a precious and chosen vessel, who shall be overshadowed and conceive by the power of the Holy Ghost, and bring forth a son, yea, even the Son of God. (Alma 7:10)

Following this introductory verse, in which the fortunate saints in Gideon learned the name of the mother of the Son of God, come a few of the most beautiful verses in scripture regarding the Atonement of Christ:

> And he shall go forth, suffering pains and afflictions and temptations of every kind; and this that the word might be fulfilled which saith he will take upon him the pains and the sicknesses of his people. And he will take upon him death, that he may loose the bands of death which bind his people; and he will take upon him their infirmities, that his bowels may be filled with mercy, according to the flesh, that he may know according to the flesh how to succor his people according to their infirmities. (Alma 7:11–12)

We all know and believe that Jesus suffered for our sins, but these precious Book of Mormon verses mention that

Jesus also took upon himself our pains, afflictions, tempta-
tions, infirmities, and even death itself. These verses expand
the reach of the Atonement of Christ beyond just our sins,
to every pain, sickness, and infirmity we feel. I cannot go too
quickly past the two verses above, since they demonstrate
another unique contribution of the Book of Mormon.

Referring to these two verses of Alma spoken to the
Saints in Gideon, Elder Jeffrey R. Holland has written:

> Most Christians believe that, based upon repentance,
> the atonement of Christ will redeem humankind from
> the final consequences of sin and death. But only those
> who receive the restored gospel, including the Book of
> Mormon, know how thoroughly the Atonement heals
> and helps with so many more categories of disappoint-
> ment and heartache here and now, in time as well as in
> eternity. In this life as well as the next, Christ "restor-
> eth my soul" and administers "goodness and mercy . . .
> all the days of my life" (Psalm 23:3, 6). (*Christ and the
> New Covenant* [1997], 113)

In the words of Elder Neal A. Maxwell, "Our sicknesses
and infirmities were borne by Him even before they were
borne by us. . . . Can we presume to teach Him who trod
'the wine-press alone' anything at all about feeling for-
saken?" (*Even As I Am* [1982], 116–17). What a thrill it
must have been for those in Gideon to be privileged to hear
such a detailed prophecy of Christ and such a thorough
explanation regarding the reach of his Atonement. Finally, I
cannot think of a more beautiful way to close an address
than the way Alma concluded his sermon in Gideon:

And now, may the peace of God rest upon you, and upon your houses and lands, and upon your flocks and herds, and all that you possess, your women and your children, according to your faith and good works, from this time forth and forever. And thus I have spoken. Amen. (Alma 7:27)

Isn't that beautiful? What a stunning contrast. Those in Zarahemla missed the prophecies of Christ that those in Gideon were prepared and privileged to hear. Message for us? Be an honorary citizen of Gideon by being spiritually prepared, and who knows what you might hear? (In addition, you may have also noticed that Alma's remarks in Gideon were less than half as long as those in Zarahemla. Do you want shorter meetings? Get your act together.)

ALMA 17: THE I-WILL-BE-THY-SERVANT MESSAGE

Does Alma's closing verse make you want to read the rest of Alma 7? Good. You know what to do. Next, what about those who know nothing about Christ? How do we help them gather?

Ammon, one of the sons of Mosiah, goes to the land of Ishmael among those who don't know about Christ. Ammon is quickly taken, bound, and brought before King Lamoni.

What should Ammon do at this point? Call them all to repentance immediately? All in good time; stand by. King Lamoni asks Ammon if it is his desire to dwell among the Lamanites. Ammon's answer is intriguing: "Yea, I desire to dwell among this people for a time; yea, and perhaps until the day I die" (Alma 17:23). Wait a minute, is Ammon incognito? Why doesn't he tell them who he is? "Hey, I'm here on a mission, and you guys need to repent, like, now!" Again, don't the scriptures say, "Say nothing but repentance unto this generation" (D&C 11:9)? Well, sure, eventually repentance will be the message, but perhaps Ammon is in a hunter mission. The scriptures also say, "Remember faith, virtue, knowledge, temperance, *patience,* brotherly kindness, godliness, charity, humility, diligence" (D&C 4:6; emphasis added). I think we can rest assured that Ammon was doing things exactly as he should because he was being guided by the Spirit of the Lord.

Ammon's presence, demeanor, countenance, or something is so impressive that King Lamoni asks if Ammon would like to take one of his daughters to wife. (You know you're making a good impression when a father asks you to date one of his daughters.) We don't know exactly how much King Lamoni knew about Ammon, but isn't it true that Ammon was a prince? He was a son of King Mosiah, right? Don't kings often arrange the marriages of their offspring with royalty from other nations to build alliances? They do. But we're getting off topic.

Ammon declines the matrimonial offer from a potential father-in-law and offers instead, "I will be thy servant" (Alma 17:25). Ammon's opportunity to gather will come soon enough. In fact, after the enemies of the king scatter the flocks, and Ammon prepares to gather them again (did you notice that? scatter, gather), Ammon teaches us all a boat-load, or more appropriately a chariot-load, when he says, "I will . . . win the hearts of these my fellow-servants, that I may lead them to believe in my words" (Alma 17:29).

There is a powerful and useful sequence in there. First, I will win their hearts; second, I will lead them to believe in my words. To some extent, as someone once said, "People must respect the messenger before they'll listen to the message." In some parts of the world, missionaries teach English classes, volunteer for community service, or do local service projects to "win hearts" with love so that they may "lead others to believe in their words."

A good friend of mine who served in a "hunter" mission heard a couple of his fellow missionaries report to the mission president, "We tracted seven hours today!" The mission president replied, "Well, you served with all your might, but not with all your mind." Whoa, that's one to think about. *Activity is not necessarily accomplishment.* Serving with all your mind may mean finding ways to get into gospel conversations with people, the kind of people in some hunter missions who would not open the door to tracting missionaries.

Getting back to our Book of Mormon story: eventually, after intense battle sequences including slings, rocks, clubs, and some literal "disarming," Ammon is brought back into the king's presence. The king asks Ammon what power he used to defend the flocks. Ammon's response is textbook: "Wilt thou hearken unto my words, if I tell thee by what power I do these things?" (Alma 18:22).

They answer that they are all ears (and probably that

they would like to keep their arms), and Ammon now has his chance. And what does he teach? I can hardly wait to tell you! Remember the three pillars of eternity back in chapter 5? Listen to this:

> Now when Ammon had said these words, he began at the *creation of the world,* and also the *creation of Adam,* and told him all the things concerning the *fall of man,* and rehearsed and laid before him the records and the holy scriptures of the people, which had been spoken by the prophets, even down to the time that their father, Lehi, left Jerusalem. . . .
>
> But this is not all; for he expounded unto them the *plan of redemption,* which was prepared from the foundation of the world; and he also made known unto them concerning the *coming of Christ,* and all the works of the Lord did he make known unto them. (Alma 18:36, 39; emphasis added)

Boom, did you see that?! The Creation, the Fall, and the Atonement, the three pillars of eternity. Eventually, King Lamoni offers humble and sincere prayer and is converted to the Lord.

By contrast, Ammon's brother Aaron, interestingly, went into the city of Jerusalem and "first began to preach" (Alma 21:4). Result? He was thrown in prison. No offer for service, no "I would like to live here," no effort to win their hearts is mentioned. Could this specific story be preserved for us for a reason? I believe so, because eventually Ammon gets his brother Aaron out of jail, and Aaron, in an audience with King Lamoni's father, says, "O king, if thou wilt spare our lives, *we will be thy servants*" (Alma 22:3; emphasis added). Did Ammon teach him that approach? Could be.

Although Ammon is no longer with his brother Aaron at this point, Ammon is still winning hearts, because King Lamoni's father asks Aaron where he is. Now, notice what Aaron teaches, and be prepared for another "boom!"

> And Aaron did expound unto him the scriptures from *the creation* of Adam, laying *the fall* of man before him, and their carnal state and also *the plan of redemption*, which was prepared from the foundation of the world, through *Christ*, for all whosoever would believe on his name. (Alma 22:13; emphasis added)

Boom! There they are again, the three pillars. The three pillars can be seen as answers to what we used to call "golden questions":

- How did we all get here? What's going on here? *The Creation.*
- If there really is a God, why is there so much death and sadness? *The Fall.*
- Is there any hope for life beyond death? *The Atonement.*

Eventually, both King Lamoni, taught by Ammon, and King Lamoni's father, taught by Aaron, were converted unto the Lord. The conversion process didn't start with a bold door approach in this case—it started with Ammon's love and his sincere desire to serve. In that same spirit, perhaps this is why the missionary anthem is "Called to Serve" rather than "Repent, Ye Heathens."

How interesting that the Book of Mormon was designed to give us ideas and principles for approaching those at different stations and in different places in their lives.

THE GATHERING BEGINS . . . WHEN?

Not only does the Book of Mormon teach and testify of the gathering of Israel, but the Book of Mormon itself is a sign that the gathering has begun.

Do you know where to find the longest sentence in the Book of Mormon? (Neither do I, but I'll bet this one is a candidate.) Start reading in 3 Nephi 21:1 and don't stop reading until you come to a period. Go ahead, I'll wait. Did you find it? Quite the long sentence, isn't it? It looks like the first period doesn't appear until the end of verse 7.

1. And verily I say unto you, I give unto you a sign, that ye may know the time when these things shall be about to take place—that I shall gather in, from their long dispersion, my people, O house of Israel, and shall establish again among them my Zion;

2. And behold, this is the thing which I will give unto you for a sign—for verily I say unto you that when these things which I declare unto you, and which I shall declare unto you hereafter of myself, and by the power of the Holy Ghost which shall be given unto you of the Father, shall be made known unto the Gentiles that they may know concerning this people who are a remnant of the house of Jacob, and

concerning this my people who shall be scattered by them;

3. Verily, verily, I say unto you, when these things shall be made known unto them of the Father, and shall come forth of the Father, from them unto you;

4. For it is wisdom in the Father that they should be established in this land, and be set up as a free people by the power of the Father, that these things might come forth from them unto a remnant of your seed, that the covenant of the Father may be fulfilled which he hath covenanted with his people, O house of Israel;

5. Therefore, when these works and the works which shall be wrought among you hereafter shall come forth from the Gentiles, unto your seed which shall dwindle in unbelief because of iniquity;

6. For thus it behooveth the Father that it should come forth from the Gentiles, that he may show forth his power unto the Gentiles, for this cause that the Gentiles, if they will not harden their hearts, that they may repent and come unto me and be baptized in my name and know of the true points of my doctrine, that they may be numbered among my people, O house of Israel;

7. And when *these things* come to pass that thy seed shall begin to know *these things*—it shall be a sign unto them, that they may know that the work of the Father hath already commenced unto the fulfill-ing of the covenant which he hath made unto the

people who are of the house of Israel. (3 Nephi
21:1–7; emphasis added)

The Book of Mormon has a few nicknames, including
the "golden plates" or the "new covenant." But within the
text itself, the words *these things* are often used to refer to
the record on the plates. For example, Moroni's promise
begins, "When ye shall receive *these things* . . ." (Moroni
10:4; emphasis added).

So, when *these things* come to light, it will be a sign
that the gathering is under way! It must be a thrill to be
converted unto the Lord, receive your patriarchal blessing,
and by revelation learn that you are part of the house of
Israel and that the Book of Mormon was a part of your
gathering.

In the Worldwide Youth Devotional referenced earlier,
Sister Wendy Nelson spoke about a meeting in Moscow,
Russia, with about 100 sisters. In that meeting, Sister
Nelson asked each of the sisters to stand and share her lin-
eage. Sister Nelson reported:

As the names of the twelve tribes of Israel were announced—from Asher to Zebulun—and as the women
stood, we were all amazed with what we were witness-
ing, feeling, and learning. How many of the twelve
tribes of Israel do you think were represented in that
small gathering of fewer than 100 women on that
Saturday in Moscow? Eleven! Eleven of the twelve tribes
of Israel were represented in that one room! The only
tribe missing was that of Levi. I was astonished. It was

a spiritually moving moment for me. ("Hope of Israel," Worldwide Youth Devotional, June 3, 2018)

Sister Nelson said that on the next day, they met an elder from the tribe of Levi. The gathering of Israel is under way, and you and I and the Book of Mormon are part of this gathering!

The gathering of Israel is about preparing ourselves and the world for the Second Coming of Christ. It is also about ministering, fellowshipping, serving in the temple, and gathering those who are on the other side of the veil. President Russell M. Nelson taught that gathering is just about anything that helps people move closer to the Lord:

> *Anytime* you do *anything* that helps *anyone*—on either side of the veil—take a step toward making covenants with God and receiving their essential baptismal and temple ordinances, you are helping to gather Israel. It is as simple as that. ("Hope of Israel," Worldwide Youth Devotional; emphasis in original)

In this chapter, I have chosen to focus on the missionary aspect of gathering as taught in the Book of Mormon. Whether as hunters or as fishers, the Lord has sent us to assist in the gathering. Whether we are working with members of the Church who are doing well, or with members who are coasting, or with people who have no knowledge of Christ at all, we are participating in the gathering. And one of our greatest tools to teach us how to be a gatherer for all people is the Book of Mormon.

THE KEYSTONE AND THE BIG ROCKS

While writing this book, I had the opportunity to visit the Holy Land. One of our stops was the ancient city of Bet Shean, one of the cities in the Decapolis. The Old Testament mentions Bet Shean as the place where the bodies of Saul and his sons, including Jonathan, were hung from the city walls (kind of gruesome—see 1 Samuel 31:10–13).

While walking through the ruins, many of which were below eye level, I noticed a tall, intact archway and stopped to take these photos:

We were surrounded by acres of 2,000-year-old ruins, most of them rubble that had fallen down (a good example of entropy), but this arch was still standing. Why? Because of the keystone—the stone at the top of the arch ingeniously designed to bear the weight of the adjacent stones. As I looked up at this majestic arch, I couldn't help but think of this statement of Joseph Smith:

> I told the brethren that the Book of Mormon was
> the most correct of any book on earth, and the keystone

of our religion, and a man would get nearer to God by abiding by its precepts, than by any other book. (*Teachings of Presidents of the Church: Joseph Smith* [2007], 64)

President Ezra Taft Benson elaborated on Joseph Smith's statement: "Just as the arch crumbles if the keystone is removed, so does all the Church stand or fall with the truthfulness of the Book of Mormon" ("The Book of Mormon—Keystone of Our Religion," *Ensign*, November 1986).

As you might remember from an earlier chapter, I often begin a semester by wondering what it might be like to have Lucy Mack Smith come and visit our class and tell us what it cost her family to bring us the Book of Mormon. Joseph Smith's name has indeed been "had for good and evil," as Moroni told him it would be (JS—H 1:33).

It's strange, but as missionaries share the restored gospel, some are willing to accept the teachings of the gospel but have a hard time with more modern revelations, such as the First Vision.

It's interesting that those who fully believe in the Bible have no problem with heavenly visitations—for example, a Jew named Saul was on the road to Damascus when he had a remarkable visionary experience. His named was changed to Paul and he became an Apostle and a powerful advocate for Christ. As Latter-day Saints, we love Paul and believe wholeheartedly in his vision. Brother Joseph Fielding McConkie commented:

If we change the name from Saul to Joseph, the time from two thousand years ago to less than two hundred years ago, and the place from Damascus to Palmyra, somehow the story becomes incredible to professed Bible believers. Virtually every missionary has heard someone say, "I would join your church if it were not for the Joseph Smith story." You would never hear anyone say, "I would be a Christian and believe the Bible if it were not for the story of Saul on the road to Damascus." (*Here We Stand* [1995], 83)

Our testimony is that the Lord is the same yesterday, today, and forever, and that the "visions and blessings of old are returning, and angels are coming to visit the earth" ("The Spirit of God," *Hymns* [1985], no. 2). Perhaps my favorite paragraph from *Preach My Gospel* discusses the fact that not only have angels come, but they've brought something with them:

Our invitation to you and all people is to add to the truths you already treasure. Consider our evidence that our Heavenly Father and His Son, Jesus Christ, have again reached out to God's children in love and revealed the fulness of the gospel to a prophet. This prophet's name is Joseph Smith. The evidence of this glorious truth is found in a book—the Book of Mormon—which you can read, ponder, and pray about. If you pray with a sincere heart, with real intent and faith in Christ, God will tell you by the power of the Holy Ghost that it is true. (*Preach My Gospel* [2004], 41–42)

Our church was not formed from just another take on the Bible, as many others have been. Our church was founded when heavenly messengers came again to the earth. Along with delivering priesthood and power and keys, they gave us 531 pages of evidence that we can read, ponder, study, search, and pray about. What will you notice as you search? An invitation, repeated over and over again. At the end of the Book of Mormon, Moroni leaves one last invitation and asks readers to "Come unto Christ, and be perfected in him" (Moroni 10:32).

A few years ago, I decided to do a scriptural search to discover how many times the "Come unto Christ" invitation occurs in the scriptures. I looked for both the phrases "Come unto Christ" and "Come unto me" (the latter occurring when Jesus was either speaking or being quoted by prophets). I discovered twenty-eight examples. But here was the stunner—guess how many of the twenty-eight invitations were in the Book of Mormon? *Twenty-five!* Twenty-five of the twenty-eight invitations to come unto Christ come from the Book of Mormon. The Book of Mormon invites, and invites, and invites again. Elder David A. Bednar observed:

> The central and recurring theme of the Book of Mormon is the invitation for all to "come unto Christ, and be perfected in him" (Moroni 10:32). The teachings, warnings, admonitions, and episodes in this remarkable book of scripture all focus upon and testify of Jesus the Christ as the Redeemer and our Savior. ("A Reservoir of Living Water," BYU Devotional, February 4, 2007)

FITTING IT ALL IN

I would like to conclude this book in the same way I conclude my Book of Mormon classes. I love to share a common analogy I first read in a book called *First Things First*.

At a time-management seminar, a presenter placed a large glass container on the table and began to fill it with large, grapefruit-sized rocks. When the rocks reached the top of the container, the presenter looked to the audience and asked, "Is it full?" The audience nodded in the affirmative, so the presenter reached underneath the table and brought forth a box of gravel. As he poured the gravel into the container, the audience realized it really hadn't been full before, as the gravel filled in the gaps between the larger rocks. "Now is it full?" he asked, and the audience laughed and said, "Uh, probably not." Sure enough, he brought another box out from under the table and poured fine sand into the container. The audience watched as the sand filled in the empty spaces. "Now is it full?" he asked, and the audience answered, "We're not so sure!" Then the presenter chuckled and poured water into the container until it rose to the brim. "Now is it full?" "Yeah," the audience responded, "we don't think you can get anything else in there!"

"Okay, so what's the point?" asked the presenter. (Keep in mind this was a time-management seminar.) The audience responded, "We get it, no matter how many things you have to do, you can always fit more stuff in between the gaps." "No, no, no!" the presenter countered strongly, "that's not it at all! The point is, *if you don't get the big rocks in first, you'll never be able to get them in later!*" (see Stephen R. Covey, A. Roger Merrill, and Rebecca R. Merrill, *First Things First,* [1994], 88–89).

A thought-provoking analogy! So, what are the big rocks in your life? What are the things that you must do each day? Facebook? Instagram? Netflix? Social media? And fit in the prayers and scripture reading later in any gaps you can find? Or should it be the other way around? I love teaching this little analogy because it always makes me reevaluate my own life. I find as a teacher I am constantly packing and repacking my bags for a guilt trip. Care to join me?

What are the big rocks in your life? We are all juggling. We are all busy, and I don't know anyone who doesn't struggle with trying to do it all—and often do it all at once. It's a daily dilemma, and I try and I fail and I try again, but one thing I know: my day goes better when scripture study is part of it. It's still stress and pressure and deadlines and endless bills. Life is still life. But I know it goes better when I spend a little time with the Savior and the Spirit.

The fact is, it's never been easier to spend time in the scriptures. With our little smartphones—pocket-sized computers that would have filled a room a few decades ago—we can listen to the scriptures and the words of the prophets almost whenever we want to. My wife listens to a general conference address almost every morning as she's getting ready for the day. In a world immersed in screens and media, much of which takes us away from God, it is more important than ever to immerse ourselves in the words of the Lord, and they are more instantly accessible to us than they have ever been.

PROMISES

In a class I took from Elder Gerald N. Lund, he explored the different methods we use to try to get people to read the scriptures. We discussed bribery—*a candy bar for anyone who read this week.* We talked about the medicine approach—*you're not going to like this, but it's good for you.* And we talked about guilt trips—*you should be reading every day, you slacker*! But Elder Lund suggested the approach the scriptures themselves use—*promises*. And he commented that most of the promised blessings for reading the scriptures pertain to this life, today, right now, not some future reward. Then he gave us the following list of references. Look them up, and list the promises yourself.

Joshua 1:8	2 Nephi 32:3	Helaman 15:7–8
Psalm 119:7	Jacob 2:8	D&C 11:21
Psalm 119:105	Alma 12:10	D&C 19:23
Romans 15:4	Alma 17:2–3	D&C 68:4
2 Timothy	Alma 31:5	D&C 84:85
3:15–17	Alma 37:44	JS–M 1:37
1 Nephi 15:24	Helaman 3:29–30	

I saved many of my college textbooks thinking I might need them someday. But over time, they each became obsolete as newer versions were published. They are all recycle-bin fodder now. But my scriptures, some of the oldest words

I have on my shelf, never go obsolete. They are still true even though some of them are thousands of years old.

LAST DAY OF CLASS

Well, the time is far spent. Fortunately, you have your own copy of the Book of Mormon, so you can pick your own favorite teachings and embark on your own journey of discovery anytime you want! When Nephi was asked what the rod of iron represented in Lehi's dream, he responded with strong words containing a promise:

> And I said unto them that it was the word of God; and whoso would hearken unto the word of God, and would hold fast unto it, they would *never perish*; neither could the temptations and the fiery darts of the adversary overpower them unto blindness, to lead them away to destruction. (1 Nephi 15:24; emphasis added)

Never is a strong word. If we hope to "never perish," we know what to do—hearken and hold fast to the word of God.

You may recall that in August 2005, President Gordon B. Hinckley challenged the members of the Church to read the entire Book of Mormon before the year was out (see "A Testimony Vibrant and True," *Ensign*, August 2005). In the subsequent months, gratitude poured out from pulpits around the world as members bore testimony of the blessings they felt in their personal lives as a result of responding to that challenge.

There is something powerful about consistency in scripture study. Our bodies need water every single day.

A five-gallon water jug, downed in one sitting only once a month, will not enable us to survive. The same is true of our spirits. The teachings and doctrines of the Book of Mormon are like "living water," but they are best experienced as daily living water providing life, refreshment, and joy to the soul. As mentioned before, with an entire gospel library contained in our smartphones, it's never been easier.

We're about to conclude. I picked a few of the doctrines and teachings I found most interesting for this book. We've talked about the plan of salvation, the fortunate fall, and the no-gaps Atonement, as well as the Resurrection, the gathering of Israel, and the Lord Jesus Christ being the object of our conversion.

BACK TO THE FIRST DAY OF CLASS

So where did we start, and how did we get here? On day one, or in the first chapter, we explored the question, "Why do we need the Book of Mormon?" The first answer is still the best—it is a second witness of Jesus Christ.

In the New Testament, the resurrected Jesus appeared to many people, including Mary Magdalene, the women who came to the tomb, the Twelve, the disciples, and, according to Paul, "above five hundred brethren" (1 Corinthians 15:6), as well as, of course, to Paul himself on the road to Damascus.

Fired by their personal experience, these witnesses fearlessly took Christ's message to the world, enduring every kind of persecution imaginable. I love to read the New

Testament and see the impact of Christ's Resurrection on those who witnessed it!

In another hemisphere, the resurrected Jesus appeared to a large multitude of 2500. Every single eye was upon him. We presume he could have simply stood in front of that large audience and given a life-changing sermon, and that would have been powerful enough! But it wasn't enough. Jesus invited the entire multitude, "one by one," not only to hear with their ears and see with their eyes but to feel in an intimate way. He said:

> Thrust your hands into my side, and . . . feel the prints of the nails in my hands and in my feet. (3 Nephi 11:14)

It's one thing to shake someone's hand and to feel your flesh touching theirs, but imagine being invited to touch someone's *wounds*. That is an intensely personal experience—an intensely sacred experience, in this case.

Jesus, on that day, created 2500 sure witnesses of his Resurrection. This emotional and powerful procession must have taken several hours. If each individual in the multitude had taken fifteen seconds to feel the Savior's hands, feet, and side, it would have taken ten hours. (That is one line we would be happy to wait in all day long.)

Imagine the impact of 2500 sure witnesses of Christ who not only heard his words but touched his hands and felt his wounds. They completely transformed Nephite society for hundreds of years.

In fact, the book of 4 Nephi, immediately following

Jesus's appearance, covers a span of nearly 300 years, yet it is only one chapter! Why is it so short? Nothing to report. The people kept the commandments and they prospered in the land, *as promised.*

It was in the third generation after Christ that things began to disintegrate. My personal opinion is that the generation who went forth "one by one" to become personal witnesses of Christ were growing old and passing away, and the power of their testimonies went with them, to some extent.

I have no memory at all of my great-grandparents. But I remember my grandparents, a couple of generations away. If they had looked me in the eye and told me, "I was there, I saw him, I felt his hands and his feet, and I know he lives," I would never, ever forget it. But that generation, the grandparents in 4 Nephi, eventually died out, and when the witnesses of Christ were gone, the society began to go downhill.

Yes, the Book of Mormon is not only a second witness of Christ as a book but a record of *thousands* of witnesses of Christ, and a witness of what their testimonies did for society. I would love to live in the place described in early 4 Nephi among all those witnesses of Christ. "Surely there could not be a happier people among all the people who had been created by the hand of God" (4 Nephi 1:16).

Four times in 4 Nephi, Mormon mentions that there was "no contention," as if he simply cannot believe it. Perhaps some readers have thought, "Maybe there weren't any in-laws back then." As if to prevent such speculation, Mormon says, "And they were married, and given in marriage" (4 Nephi 1:11), and yet, "there was no contention among all the people" (4 Nephi 1:13).

How did they do it? The answer, I believe, lies in 4 Nephi 1:15: "There was no contention in the land, because of the love of God which did dwell in the hearts of the people." When those 2500 souls went forth to feel the wound in his side and to touch his hands and feet, they most certainly felt his love—his perfect, consuming, divine love—and "the love of God" stayed with them and changed them forever.

Jesus taught, "Greater love hath no man than this, that a man lay down his life for his friends" (John 15:13). This most fortunate multitude actually felt Jesus's hands, literally holding in their own hands the physical evidence that he had lain down his life for them.

One of the wonderful things about scripture study is that we may vicariously feel what those in the scriptures felt. As we read the Book of Mormon, this reservoir of golden answers that is, above all else, Another Testament of Jesus Christ, we get to stand in line with the 2500. And when we approach our study with prayerful, grateful hearts, we may feel His love as well.

This love of God will sustain us in this challenging world and give us hope and courage to press on until the promised day when Jesus will come again. On that most glorious occasion, it is my belief that we too will be invited to feel the wound in his side, and to feel his hands and feet and, without question, his overwhelming love—not vicariously, and not as part of a group or multitude, but in person, one by one.

ABOUT THE AUTHOR

JOHN BYTHEWAY served a mission to the Philippines and later graduated from Brigham Young University. He has a master's degree in religious education and is a part-time instructor at the BYU Salt Lake Center. John is the author of many bestselling books, audio talks, and DVDs, including *How Do I Know if I Know?*; *Isaiah for Airheads*; and *Righteous Warriors: Lessons from the War Chapters in the Book of Mormon*. He and his wife, Kimberly, have six children.